Seven Secrets To Enlightened Happiness

Your Guide To The Life You Were Meant To Live

Alan Allard, Ph.D.

Copyright © 2015 Alan Allard, Ph.D.

All rights reserved.

ISBN-13: 9781481961820

DEDICATION

To Dee Dee, my wife and high school sweetheart: Thank you for your unfailing support in the writing of this book and for your years of love, friendship and creativity. You are beautiful, smart and incredibly talented. "Carentondon."

To my two daughters, Dana and Jamie: I could not be more proud of you. You are both amazing—in every sense of the word and I love you more than words can convey.

To my two sons-in-law, Jonathan and Greivin: How did I get so lucky? I love and respect both of you and I am so happy we are family.

To Dorothy Weathers Allard: Mom, your poems are full of wit and surprise, just like you. You have never stopped learning, growing and changing. You are an inspiration to everyone.

To JoAnn Corley, President, The Human Sphere: Thank you for your friendship over many years and your relentless encouragement for me to write this book and for your enthusiasm in promoting it.

CONTENTS

Preface: You Are Wired For Happiness	i
Introduction: This Way to Happiness	Pg 1
Secret One: Your Beliefs Create Your Reality	Pg 5
Secret Two: Your Inner Vision Is the Mental Blueprint For Your Reality	Pg 43
Secret Three: Master Your Self-Talk Master Your Life	Pg 63
Secret Four: Self-Confidence Fuels Your Success	Pg 83
Secret Five: There Is No Substitute For Self-Love	Pg 97
Secret Six: Gratitude Is the Great Happiness Multiplier	Pg 113
Secret Seven: Action Fuels Your Happiness	Pg 122
Bonus Chapter: How to Rise Above Your Circumstances	Pg 129
Wrapping Up	Pg 133
My Gift to You	Pg 135
Suggested Resources	pg 137

What Alan's Clients are Saying	Pg 139
About Alan	Pg 144

PREFACE

You came into this world with the ability to know what you want, to live from purpose and to connect deeply with others. You were born to be audacious and to take action on your vision for how you want your life to be. In short, you came into this world capable of creating incredible happiness for yourself.

If that's so, why do so many people settle for far less than they truly want? There isn't just one answer to that question. However, what happens in our early formative years explains a lot. As children we learned to question who we are, doubt our true worth and capabilities and fear the opinions and judgments of others.

In our attempts to be loved and to be accepted we began to question our place in the world and our worth. We internalized the criticism we heard from others and we began to fear mistakes and failures. The end result is self-doubt:

"What if I'm rejected, not liked or loved?"

"What if I go for my dream and end up broke?"

"What if I take some risks at work and in life and I fail?"

"What if I'm honest about what I want in life but don't believe I can have what I want?"

Despite our fears and self-doubts, our capacity to thrive in life is real—more than most of us realize. You can change your life and transform it into anything you *truly* want. I'm not saying there aren't any real limits in life—there are. It takes a certain level of I.Q. to be a brain surgeon or a nuclear physicist. So yes, you do have some limitations.

However, too many people focus on what they can't have or do instead of what they can have or do. That keeps them from unleashing their powerful self. We're all capable of learning how to be more successful, more fulfilled and yes, happier.

I know that to be true from my own life and from over twenty years of working with clients—first as a psychotherapist and now as an executive coach and consultant and as a transformative life coach for individuals and couples.

The bottom line is you can change your life and career trajectory more than you know. It won't happen overnight—but you can start today. As a former psychotherapist in private practice in the Chicago suburbs, I worked with hundreds of clients over a span of twelve years. They came into my office because they wanted something in their life to change.

My clients said things like, "I'm depressed," "My anxiety is getting worse," "My marriage is falling apart" or "I want to find out what I want to do when I grow up." That's what they *said*. But what did they *want*?

Ultimately they wanted what we all want—to be happy or to feel happy more consistently. As a therapist, I was trained to diagnose my clients and to give them a place to talk about their pain. Thankfully, I soon discovered a faster way to help my clients create the happiness, fulfillment and life success they wanted. That faster way was hearing and affirming my client's pain and then helping them to *focus on what they wanted as soon as possible.*

I helped them to understand a simple but profound principle: Our *"problems" are messages from life that something needs to change.* When something isn't ideal in our life, that's a clue it's time to change what we're thinking and what we're doing. I will help you to do just that, one step at a time.

You will find coaching tips and coaching exercises throughout the book. You can do them when you first read them or you can read the book first and then do the exercises. The focus of this book is *Enlightened Happiness* and how to design and create more enlightened happiness, meaning and fulfillment in your life.

Why is this focus important, especially if you're going through challenges you want to get rid of? Because the best way to deal with what you don't want is to shift your focus and put your energy on what you do want.

My coaching, speaking and workshops aren't about getting rid of your "problems" or unwanted circumstances. My focus is about transforming yourself and becoming the architect and builder of the life you want and deserve. It's about knowing you were designed to be happy and to *thrive* in all areas of your life.

To thrive in life requires what I call *Enlightened Happiness*. But what is that?

- *Enlightened* refers to higher levels of intellectual, emotional and spiritual thoughts, beliefs and actions ("Spiritual" means anything related to love and to the human spirit).
- *Happiness* is feeling **positive energy** about yourself and your life, or feeling positive energy about the progress you're making.

I make a distinction between *Enlightened Happiness* and happiness because there are things we do at times to feel "happy" that have unintended consequences. In other words, what makes you "happy" for a brief time ends up causing you disappointment, frustration and pain.

Enlightened Happiness means thinking about the short-term **and** the long-term impact of our values, choices and behaviors. It involves thinking ahead and playing our mental movies out as far as we can to ask if we like how the movie unfolds. Will the choices we make and the actions we take create lasting happiness?

Here are some common ways we might settle for what we mistake for "happiness" instead of listening to our Higher Self (the part of you that is always connected to the source of positive energy, whatever you might think that to be) and living a life of *Enlightened Happiness*:

- Keeping your dreams on the back burner or burying them under busyness, distractions or fears.
- "Emotional eating"—using food (or anything else pleasurable in the moment) to feel good and distract yourself or numb yourself from emotions you would rather not feel.
- Saying "Yes" to someone when you really want to say "No."
- Not setting boundaries with others.
- Procrastination—gaining temporary relief that you pay for later.
- Staying in your comfort zone—failing to challenge yourself.
- Spending more money now than wisdom would suggest and failing to save and invest for the future.
- Ignoring "relationship issues" because it's the easy thing to do for now.

- Settling in a relationship because it's easier to stay in it than end it.

These are examples of *unenlightened* happiness—doing what feels comfortable or good now without considering future consequences.

Enlightened Happiness is a way of thinking and pattern of behavior that pays off both now and down the road as well. It's like saving money now, getting the short-term benefit of increased savings and also getting the future benefits of compound interest.

That's what happens with *Enlightened Happiness*—the first choice or action rewards us immediately and then continues to do so in a compounding effect over time. I call it Compound Happiness.

It's also important to know that if you want to be happier, more fulfilled and more in love with life, you can have all that now—you don't have to wait for your outer circumstance to change for the "better."

You can be happier now by replacing rigid beliefs about how things **should** be, **ought to** be or **have to** be with more useful perspectives. You can be happier by unconditionally accepting whatever is in your life now and by accepting yourself now, while pursuing all you want to be and all you want to have.

Enlightened Happiness is about accepting that which we have no direct control over and using it to gain a deeper and richer understanding of self and of life. *Enlightened Happiness* is about believing we are more capable and far more powerful than we know.

Instead of being hypnotized by circumstances, we can see beyond them and audaciously look into the future through the lenses of curiosity, courage and creativity. *Enlightened Happiness* allows us to celebrate small changes and progress knowing that small successes lead to bigger successes. Because of that, *Enlightened Happiness* is the antidote to perfectionism.

Finally, *Enlightened Happiness* comes from knowing we create both happiness and unhappiness from within—and knowing that what we pay attention to grows. If you pay more attention to the times you feel happy, content, fulfilled, motivated, grateful, and loved, you will find your happiness growing.

Now that we have an understanding of *Enlightened Happiness*, let me ask you a question: When it comes to your happiness, which of the following statements do you relate to the most?

- "I'm happy, but..."

You are happy, but you believe there are some things getting in the way and you would like to transcend them—and live from a whole different level of happiness.

For instance, is your happiness hijacked when something goes wrong, when you make a mistake, or when you compare yourself to someone else more "successful" or think about your finances?

- "I will be happier when 'X' changes."

You are happy with yourself or your life…until you think about something in your life you wished was better. For instance, your weight, your income, a relationship you are in, being single, and so on.

This is one of the most common reasons we are not happier—we haven't learned how to be happier right now—before life "gets better." Why not learn how to add more happiness into your life now and use that positive energy to make changing your life easier and faster?

- "I'm happy with some aspects of my life, but not so happy with other areas of my life."

It's not that you are mired in unhappiness, but you feel

frustrated in some areas of your life more often than you would like. You can learn to tap into the positive energy of some areas of your life to rethink and transform other areas of your life.

I believe we were meant to be happy and that we can design and create more happiness if we know how.

Knowing how to create more happiness and fulfillment begins with understanding what Helen Keller taught:

> "Happiness cannot come from without; it comes from within."

Of course, there's more to Enlightened Happiness than what we've covered so far. *Seven Secrets To Enlightened Happiness* is your guide to living the life you are meant to live and that you know deep down you are capable of living. After all, as singer Keb Mo says, "Everybody's got a right to feel happy!"

Decide now to nourish your inner happiness—by learning how, just like you have learned so many other things in your life. At one time, you didn't know how to talk, walk, feed yourself, dress yourself, ride a bike or drive a car. However, you likely do all these things now—without even thinking about them, because you took the time to learn how to do them.

You can learn how to be at peace with yourself, how to set and achieve meaningful goals, how to have loving relationships, how to do work that you love and so on.

The good news is that you know more about being happy than you might think—and at the same time, there are things you can easily learn and implement to increase your happiness, confidence and sense of fulfillment.

ALAN ALLARD, Ph.D.

INTRODUCTION:
THIS WAY TO HAPPINESS!

Just how important is happiness? It's a simple question that only you can answer for yourself. However, simple questions aren't necessarily easy to answer. The Dalai Lama said "I believe that the very purpose of life is to be happy." Yet, Ralph Waldo Emerson disagreed and said, "The purpose of life *isn't* to be happy."

If you search the topic of happiness on the internet you will find many psychologists, religious leaders and coaches that tell us the pursuit of happiness is misguided. They tell us we should seek things other than happiness such as purpose or meaning in life.

What do you think about that?

Even if you decide happiness isn't the purpose of life and shouldn't be your top priority, my bet is you would like to be happier. But what leads to real happiness? Donald Trump seems to equate happiness with wealth, power and attention while Bill and Melinda Gates run a foundation to help others. It raises the question, "Which way to happiness?"

Does your happiness depend on getting more for

yourself or on you giving more to others? Or maybe that's a trick question and increasing your happiness involves both. Why should we have to choose between the two?

What does it take to make happiness *a way of life?* Many of us think more money is part of the equation. Despite the evidence that money can't buy happiness, we still can't keep from thinking of what it *can* buy—not to mention the bills it would pay off.

If you're in a lot of debt and you suddenly get the money to pay it all off, I'm sure you'd feel happier for a while—but for how long? In one way, life would have just gotten easier, no doubt about that. That makes it easy to think, "The more money I get, the happier I will be."

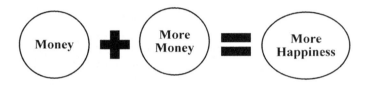

You probably know that more money doesn't necessarily translate into more happiness, love and fulfillment. In fact, it can do the opposite. It depends upon our beliefs about money, self and worthiness.

Some would tell you that if you downsized your house, car and wardrobe and lived the "minimalist" lifestyle, you would be happier. Their philosophy is "Less is more!" On the other hand, the "health and wealth" evangelists proclaim that it is your birthright to be healthy and wealthy—in fact, more is better!

Meanwhile, author and prosperity teacher Randy Gage tells us that it's a "sin" to be poor. "Sin," according to Gage is defined as "missing the mark." What is your reaction to that? The point isn't whether you agree or disagree with that statement—or anything I offer you.

The point is, "Can you suspend your current beliefs

long enough to entertain a different perspective and give it objective and honest consideration?" That's easier said than done, no doubt about it, but we can all do it.

Beyond the debate about money and possessions boosting happiness, many think the answer lies in finding their "soul mate." There are plenty of books and coaches that will tell you finding the right person will somehow "complete" your life: "If you find your soul mate, you will find your bliss."

But wait—someone else comes along and tells you that you aren't happy because you're self-centered—you selfish thing! According to this thinking, happiness is to be found in giving, not getting. We all admire Mother Theresa, but there's more to the story.

What about your own needs? We've all heard, "It's more blessed to give than to receive"—but what does that mean? After all, burnout is a serious challenge for professional "caregivers" such as therapists, doctors, nurses, clergy, medical missionaries and teachers. For many, their non-stop giving doesn't lead to happiness and health—it leads to unhappiness and health problems.

With so much conflicting and confusing information and advice out there, what can you do? You can figure it out for yourself… but you don't have to do it all *by* yourself. I'm going to help you rethink what you know about happiness and what it takes for *you* to thrive in life.

SECRET ONE: YOUR BELIEFS CREATE YOUR REALITY

*"People are not disturbed by things,
but by the view they take of them." - Epictetus*

*"We see the world, not as it is, but as we are – or, as we are
conditioned to see it." - Stephen Covey, Ph.D.*

*"If you don't like the reality you have, create a different one."
- Alan Allard*

The first secret to *Enlightened Happiness* is both simple and profound: **Your Beliefs Create Your Reality**. This "secret" has been around for ages but few have mastered it. Why is that? One reason is few people *really* believe it. When is the last time you heard someone say, "I created the situation I'm in."? For most people, outside forces explain why their lives are the way they are.

If you want to radically change any aspect of your life, ask yourself what you *really* believe about this first secret. Not what you think you believe or want to believe, but what you actually believe now. How would you know what you believe? You know by how you *feel* about any circumstance in your life and by the results you see in your life.

I say that because if you believe your beliefs create your reality, then you know you can change anything in your life. Not instantly, but with courage, vision, action and faith, you can transform your current reality into the reality you want and deserve.

If you feel overwhelmed or stuck in some way, it's because you believe your situation is beyond your ability to transform. You might be telling yourself, "I can change this" but that's just your conscious mind talking—otherwise you would feel hopeful instead of stuck and overwhelmed. If you've been feeling stuck for a while, what you believe (on a deeper level) is that nothing much is going to change.

Understanding that your beliefs create your reality changes everything. So why do so few people really believe this first secret? Here's one key reason: This secret can seem like it "blames the victim." For instance, what if you have a serious health problem? Did you bring that on yourself? What if your company lays you and thousands of others off—did you do that to yourself?

What if a drunk driver crashes into you and paralyzes you—did you create that reality from your beliefs? If you have a family member or significant other that treats you badly, did you bring that on yourself—did your beliefs create that reality?

With all these things, the question is, "What are you responsible for or not responsible for in terms of any given situation in your life?" Is it all on you? Is it partly on you? Or is it all on outside forces or other people in your life?

These are reasonable questions. The fact is there are some things we bring directly upon ourselves. We know that. Sometimes we make choices that create problems for ourselves. However, sometimes there are outside forces that shape part of our current reality. Imagine a tornado destroys your house or your CEO runs your company into bankruptcy. You didn't create those things through your beliefs or thoughts. So what does it mean that your beliefs create your reality?

It means that you directly create most of what's in your life. Beyond that, your response to what happens outside your control creates your *current reality*. Take Helen Keller for example—about two years after being born she became blind and deaf as a result of an illness. That permanent loss became her reality. However, she changed her *current reality* by how she responded to things that happened beyond her control.

When I say we create our reality from our beliefs, I mean that even when something happens outside our control, we are responsible for what we do next. What we do with what we have creates our *Current Reality*. We don't get to choose all the cards we're dealt but we do choose how we play those cards. So, what do you do after something "bad" happens outside of your control? You choose how you will respond to it.

What happens to you outside your control isn't your fault. However, it is your responsibility to choose how you respond to it.

If we want a different reality than the one we have now, we have to own the fact we've created the *Current Reality* we're living by the choices we make in response to everything in our life, even the things outside our control. After all, if you can't see how you used your power to create whatever *Current Reality* you have now, how can you use your power to create a better life?

The answer is you can't—and that can be challenging to accept, much less to embrace. I'm not talking about *saying* you believe you create your *current reality*—I'm talking about believing that on the level you boldly *demonstrate it in your life*.

In 1902 James Allen wrote the classic *As a Man*

Thinketh and stated **"Men are anxious to improve their circumstances, but are unwilling to improve themselves."** This is important because you can't directly change your circumstances. You can, however, change them indirectly by changing yourself first.

What James Allen (and other men and women who had genius insight into the human spirit) taught gets to the heart of the matter. Allen's writing both wakes us up and inspires us. It's as someone once said, "The truth will set you free, but first it will make you miserable." That, of course, isn't true all the time—but it is true some of the time.

It's always easier to blame others or things outside of ourselves such as our company, our manager, our significant other or the economy. In other words, "I would do better but I can't because..."

When we think that way we're blaming outside forces and giving up our power to create the change we want. The truth is, very few things in life can't be improved upon and changed. You can't change your age but you can change what you believe your age (or anything else) means to you.

James Allen opened my mind when I read his book as a teenager. My thinking was also shaped by Amelia Earhart when I read about her adventures. She refused to accept the limits society placed upon her in her quest to make her mark in the male dominated world she lived in.

My thinking and my beliefs were also influenced by Helen Keller taught me. Her story amazed me and I discovered that when we allow someone to teach us we can light up our world and the world around us. I wonder what would have happened to Helen Keller if she had turned her teacher away? I don't know, but what I do know is she learned to transform herself and her life.

I didn't learn about Helen Keller and Amelia Earhart from my graduate studies in psychology and counseling. I found them on my own as a teenager. I also learned much from the disciplines of theology and metaphysics that stirred my thinking. In my studies I discovered we're all talking about the same thing; the human condition and human potential.

Of course, each discipline has its own language. Psychology talks about "mental constructs," "cognitive processes," "positive expectancy," "self-efficacy," "placebo," "self-fulfilling prophecy" and "locus of control."

These are important things to know about, understand and use in our lives. However, whether we're using psychological, medical, theological or metaphysical terms, the point is we're talking about the power of the human mind and spirit.

If you want to be more proactive in life, to disrupt the status quo and to transform your life, the place to begin is with the power within you and with your thoughts and beliefs. They are the source of your creative energy, choices, actions and the results you create in your life.

You might be thinking, "But Alan, that's so basic and I've heard all that before." Yes, you're right. It *is* basic. However, my experience is few of us have mastered the basics—even when we think we have. Master the basics first and then you are able to go to the next level and then to the next and so on. *That's how you change your life.*

For instance, before you can do what a black belt martial artist does, you have to master what a white belt can do, then you master what a yellow belt can do, then you master what an orange belt can do. You can't skip the lower belts on your way to becoming a black belt martial artist. So let's start with mastering the basics—how you think and how you can use the power of beliefs to change your reality.

You can't change your *entire* life today but **you can begin to change the direction of your life today.** Think about something in your life you would like to change but haven't yet. Why is that?

It's likely you believed it was too difficult. Or perhaps you had conflicting beliefs. To change, you have to have enough of your beliefs aligned so you don't unintentionally sabotage yourself. You not only have to believe you *can* do something (self-efficacy)—you have to believe and feel you are worthy of what you want.

I am thinking now of someone who wants to be happier but is stuck in making some changes. Why is that? Because she thinks if she gets what she wants some important people in her life will be unhappy with her. She is afraid to set boundaries with them, say no to them when she needs to and she (unknowingly) feels responsible for their happiness.

Can you see from this example the role of your beliefs in growing your happiness? Everything comes from your beliefs—the choices you make, the actions you take or don't take, the risks you take and the emotional energy you have or don't have to create the life you want and deserve. Beliefs might not be everything but they are at the center of things.

So what exactly is a belief? A belief is *trust or confidence in something*. If you don't get anything else from me, get this: Your beliefs are more powerful than you realize. Why do I say that?

Because **whatever you believe to be true becomes your reality**. That means if you want to change your life, you must *start* with your beliefs. You can't change or improve your life with the beliefs that got you where you are now. Think about that statement before you move on, because *if you're struggling in some area, that means you have to get some new beliefs*.

I help my clients grasp the fact that their beliefs and their self-talk create their reality. I help them to own the fact they are the creative force in their life. When you get that, you will get all the things in life you want and deserve.

If you are willing to accept that you are the creative force in your life—and that you have potential and power you haven't discovered yet, extraordinary things are possible. You really are the Cause behind the results in your life.

That's why it's vital to do the "inner work" that enables you to create the results you want for your life. Imagine what your life would be like as you learn how to access and unleash the power you intuitively know you have. Whether life is flowing smoothly for you now or it's challenging you, you can learn to think and live from a more powerful place.

When you embrace the truth you are the creative force and the Cause behind your results you will find a source of energy you didn't realize you have. It will be inspiring, liberating and amazing. Interestingly enough, despite the fact we make our own choices, we make our choices from what we've learned and from the influences of our environment.

Much of what we've learned and what we hear and see in our environment is what can be described as a victim mentality. Instead of being taught we're powerful beyond measure we are taught there are forces beyond our control and we should just settle for what we have and be happy with it. The antidote to this thinking is to own your creative power to create a life that is deeply fulfilling and extraordinary.

The people in your life, the economy, your boss, your family and friends and your current circumstances don't determine the results your life or your happiness and fulfillment in life. They are influencers but you are the most powerful force in your life. Few people really believe that—although most think they do.

If you believe the power to shape your life resides within you and therefore not in outside forces, you have what psychology describes as *an internal locus of control*.

Someone with an internal locus of control:
- Is more likely to take personal responsibility
- Is more optimistic and action oriented
- Ventures outside their comfort zone more often
- Takes more risks
- Is more persistent in the face of challenges
- Has more fulfilling relationships

On the other hand, if you have an external locus of control, you believe that outside factors (the economy, your significant other, your boss, fate, etc.) determine what happens in your life. An external locus of control mindset is a "Victim" mindset and an internal locus of control mindset is an "Ownership" mindset.

Why is this so important? Because if you believe nothing can or will change for the better, *you will subconsciously make that your reality*. However, if you believe you are the change agent in your life, you can and *will* bring about the change you want. That's how powerful your beliefs are. They are powerful because:

Whatever you believe, *you are always right*.

That would be one way to state what we call the self-fulfilling prophecy. As Claude Bristol wrote in *The Magic of Believing*, "The subconscious mind always brings to reality what it is led to believe." The question is, "Does your subconscious mind have the beliefs it needs to create the results in life you want?"

What you need to know about your subconscious mind is once it accepts a belief it's designed to create the results that match that belief. If your subconscious believes you are worthy, capable and creative, your life will reflect those beliefs.

I will help you to believe (to feel confident) you are the creative force in your life. As you read this book, you can begin to question old beliefs that no longer serve you and you can take on new beliefs to reinvent yourself and change anything you want. As you change your beliefs, everything will change with them.

Albert Einstein is attributed as saying, "We cannot solve our problems with the same level of thinking that created them." That means you can't create a new life with the same level of thinking you created your current life from. If you want better results in your life you have to get better beliefs.

When we talk about beliefs we have to make a distinction between what our conscious mind believes and what our subconscious mind believes. Your subconscious beliefs are far more important than your conscious beliefs—and the two can be at odds with one another. Meaning, you can believe one thing consciously and believe the opposite on a subconscious level. This explains why someone will say they want to achieve something and then fail at it.

If you want greater success, fulfillment and happiness in life you have to work on the level of your deeper, subconscious beliefs. What you believe on a conscious level isn't the determining factor in your life. The determining factor is what you think and what you believe in your subconscious mind.

When the conscious mind and the subconscious mind are in conflict, the subconscious mind will win out over the course of time.

How many people do you know that wish they were in a better job, say they want a better relationship with their significant other or that they want to "lose weight"? Yet nothing changes. That's because there's a conflict between their conscious and subconscious minds. Their conscious mind says "I want to lose weight" and their subconscious mind says, "I need to keep doing what I'm doing because it gives me what I want—to feel comfortable and safe."

So how do you know what your subconscious beliefs are? The fact is there are clues everywhere. Your real beliefs, your subconscious beliefs, are always showing up in your external life. How so? Look at your paycheck, your position in your company, the quality of your relationships and your health and nutrition habits. These are all manifestations of your how you think and what you believe on a subconscious level.

You cannot outperform what your subconscious mind believes you are capable of or worthy of. At least not for any extended period of time. Your subconscious beliefs will always bring you back to their level. To get beyond your current results in life you need to go beyond your current beliefs, assumptions and thinking.

You have an opportunity every day to go beyond your current beliefs by gently influencing your

subconscious mind to accept empowering beliefs that will create and nurture the life you want. Reading this book over and over again will help you do that.

With that said, here's some good news about your beliefs—you don't have to "let go" of any old beliefs or eliminate any of your "negative" or "limiting" beliefs. You can simply take on new beliefs that empower you. It's like planting new seeds in your garden and then making sure the new seeds get what they need to flourish and thrive.

Sometimes clients ask me, "But aren't my negative beliefs like weeds in a garden? Don't I need to pull them up?" No, you don't. Your subconscious mind is like a garden in some ways and different in other ways. With a garden, you need to eliminate the weeds.

But with your subconscious mind, you can focus all your attention on tending to your useful, empowering beliefs and they will make the "weeds" a non-issue. The key is to focus on gaining new thoughts and beliefs that are consistent with the life you want. You can do that. One way to do that is to suspend your judgment on beliefs and perspectives that right now seem to be wrong or even scary.

Not many people are willing to do that. They want to keep the same beliefs they currently have because they seem to be "right." Yet think about what Aristotle said:

"It is the mark of an educated mind to be able to entertain a thought without accepting it."

Most people can't do that when it comes to a belief that contradicts one of their core beliefs about self or life. If you want to change your life, learn to entertain beliefs that contradict what you already believe. That's the beginning of the process of taking on new beliefs.

The fact that you can take on new beliefs and therefore change your life is exhilarating when you think about it. It's better than being able to mentally teleport yourself from one location to another, as fun as that would be. Changing your beliefs transports you from one place to another.

You can go from a place of doubt to confidence, from frustration to happiness, from confusion to clarity—on purpose. In fact, you already do that! Now it's a matter of learning how to do that by conscious choice. Remember, your life will change as fast as your beliefs change.

This is especially true when it comes to who you think you are, what you think you're worth and what you think you're capable of becoming and achieving. I know that from experience, because as a former psychotherapist, and now as a life coach and executive coach, I help clients change how they see themselves, their circumstances and their life.

Clients come into my office convinced their way of seeing things makes perfect sense—and they're right. From their perspective, their beliefs make perfect sense. However, I ask my clients, "Would you be willing to consider other ways of looking at this if it helped you get what you want?" Another question I ask my clients is, "Do you want to be right or do you want to be happier and more effective?"

If your beliefs about money, work, or your body and health aren't making you happy and prosperous, do you want to protect and defend those beliefs? We tend to do that out of habit. Until we disrupt our automatic, subconscious thinking, we'll continue to protect what we currently believe.

If you want better relationships, greater financial security, more confidence and deeper happiness, you might consider (once again) that **your current beliefs can't give you more than they've already given you.** That's because our beliefs are like a thermostat that regulates the temperature in a room. If the temperature changes, the thermostat's job is to bring it back to the temperature it's programmed to maintain.

Your beliefs either help you to change your circumstances or to keep them where they are now. If you want to transcend your circumstances, you have to change the way you think about and respond to them. Victor Frankl, M.D. learned this in the harshest of circumstances. Dr. Frankl was a Jewish psychiatrist who was imprisoned along with his parents and sister in Nazi concentration camps in World War II and he was the lone survivor of his family.

In *Man's Search for Meaning*, Dr. Frankl stated, **"Every human right and dignity can be taken away from a person except one, the ability to choose our response in any given situation; to choose our own way."**

Think about how you are viewing your current circumstances in life and what you say to yourself about them. Whenever you think about a circumstance or event in your life, you tell yourself a "story" about it. Your story is how you view the circumstance you think about. For instance, you have a story for why your overall life is the way it is now.

You also have stories about the specifics in your life— your relationships, your health, your financial state, your potential and so on. Your stories make sense to you and you think they're accurate and factual.

However, we create our stories from our beliefs (mistaking them for facts) and our stories either open our eyes or act as blinders. If you don't like how something in your life looks, change how you look at it by changing your story about it.

In my work as a psychotherapist, some of my clients have dealt with things most of us don't ever want to even think about. For instance, "Janet" came to me in a wheelchair telling me she had a year and a half to live after being diagnosed with Lou Gehrig's disease. Her medical doctors in Chicago were among the best money could buy and they were doing all they could for her on a physical level. However, they weren't equipped to help her on other levels.

The first thing Janet told me was, "I'm going to die

soon and there's nothing you or I can do about that." What do you think she was trying to accomplish by saying that? She was trying to do at least two things:

First, she was challenging me to see how I would respond. Next, she was asking me for help even though she was afraid I couldn't help her. That took immense courage. I would like to say I helped Janet, but I didn't. She believed she couldn't have a richer and fuller life because of her illness. That not only made what she was dealing with worse, it took a toll on her husband and friends.

Why am I telling you about Janet and my other clients throughout this book? Because I want you to know that whatever you are dealing with, you can transform your life more than you realize. You can turn your times of challenge and crisis into a time to reassess everything you "know" about yourself and everything you know about life.

There are times you might cry and doubt your ability to change your situation—that's human. But you don't have to stop there. You can emerge from your despair having discovered you're more powerful than you know. However, you might not want to think about transforming yourself and your life right now if you're hurting and struggling.

That's understandable. Take a minute and be honest with yourself because anything less won't work. **Being in denial about what you think and what you feel will never get you what you want. Awareness and acceptance is the beginning of all change. You can't change what you resist and deny.**

We know that communication is key when it comes to change in any arena of life—be it work, family or with yourself. Telling yourself things are great when you're feeling angry or afraid isn't in your best interest. It will keep you from the extraordinary life you want.

I have had some clients tell me they only want to focus

on positive things because they don't want to "feed the negative." What they don't realize is their fear of being honest with themselves makes them prisoners of their fears. As has been said, "What you resist persists." Buckminster Fuller, a 20th century inventor and visionary stated, *"You can't change anything by fighting or resisting it. You change something by making it obsolete through superior methods."*

Applying Fuller's wisdom to your emotional life means accepting all your emotions and listening to what they are teaching you. When you're feeling angry or overwhelmed that's okay. Learn to accept and embrace these emotions for what they are—what you're feeling for now. That's often hard for my clients to do without help. Why is that?

We've been taught that certain emotions are "negative." We try to keep negative things out of our life and so we try to keep the "negative" emotions out as well. Doing that gives us the *illusion* that we're being "positive," when in fact, we're not. Denial creates an internal conflict that shows up in our lives in some way.

Another reason we repress or suppress our "negative" emotions is because we don't want to feel weak. We've been taught that strong people don't experience depression, sadness or fear. So we put on a smile and say, "I'm doing fine." We haven't really bought into the fact that it takes real strength to be honest.

Being honest about "negative" emotions requires trusting that you can handle them. Many of my clients come to me fearing their "negative" emotions. They're afraid if they allow themselves to feel them they will be consumed by them. Trusting yourself to experience your "negative" emotions means taking responsibility for them. But that doesn't mean blaming yourself for anything.

Blaming yourself isn't taking responsibility—even if it seems to be. What does it mean to take responsibility?

It means you see yourself as being *Response-able*—having the ability to respond to the challenge at hand. That includes having the ability to feel whatever you might feel at the moment. If you block out your emotions you can't learn from them and use them transform your life.

If you feel stuck and hopeless in a situation, that's okay—it's just a feeling; it's not your fate. You can know that while you're in the process of improving your beliefs or behaviors, you can acknowledge and accept any emotions you have along the way.

I say all that (and will come back to it later) to reduce the amount of internal conflict you might have. For now, tell yourself, "Even though I'm feeling I can't change this situation, I will continue to support myself in creating the life I want." That way you can be honest about what you're thinking and feeling while creating an inner environment for change.

Coaching Assignment: Choose something you've been feeling overwhelmed by and say to yourself, "Even though I'm really upset about _____ I accept and love myself unconditionally."

You can change your thinking and any belief you have had up until now. But how do you do that? Have you ever wondered why so many people have a hard time changing their thinking and their beliefs? Or why *you* have had difficulty changing *your* beliefs at times?

A major reason is because when we learned our core beliefs growing up we accepted what we learned as "truth" or facts. Early in life, you had "authority figures" such as your parents and you absorbed their thinking and beliefs as "the way it is"—or as facts of life.

As adolescents or young adults we end up with the beliefs we shape our lives from and we accept them as the truth about the matter. Think about your beliefs and perspectives on religion, race issues, politics, sexuality or money. Think about your beliefs about yourself, your capabilities and your self-worth. Where did they come from?

How many of your beliefs are "inherited beliefs?" Could it be that to some extent you're living a "hand me down life" without realizing it? Which of your beliefs serve as fuel for your success and well-being and which ones place unnecessary limits on your life?

For instance, you may have heard messages like, "Do you think money grows on trees?" "Why aren't you ever satisfied with what you have?" "Why can't you just do like you're told?" "I think you should become a doctor—that way you will never have to worry about making a good living."

Many of us learned such beliefs so well we accepted them as truth and facts.

Coaching Assignment: Write down two beliefs you learned growing up that might not be serving you today:

1._____

2._____

Or maybe the messages weren't so blunt—they were more subtle. We don't just take in what people say directly, we also absorb what they communicate more subtly. For instance, one thing that might have been implied is the message, "What I'm telling you is the way it is." That doesn't teach you to own your thinking and your beliefs—it teaches you to give your power to another person.

Think about whether your parents ever had a discussion with you about money, sex, religion or any other important topic and said, "Here are my beliefs on this, but remember, they're just *my beliefs*. I got them from my parents, who got them from their parents, who got them from..."

Did your mom or dad or other influencers in your life ever tell you, "What I'm telling you is something I've carefully thought through and this is what I believe for now. If it makes sense to you, use it. But remember to re-evaluate it along the way to make sure it's your own thinking, not mine."

Few children have the benefit of someone telling them that all the beliefs they are absorbing, subconsciously or otherwise, are merely someone's opinion. They aren't told that one of the most important things they can do throughout their life is to examine and question all their beliefs to see if those beliefs will lead to more happiness, fulfillment and meaning in life.

Instead, what is likely to be heard by a child growing up is the silent message, "This is the truth, end of story." The child isn't taught that what they just heard is their parent's *story*—their explanation of things. So the child takes it all in as if it were the truth on the matter, not to be questioned, much less disputed.

The end result is we grow up learning what to believe and how to think about certain things and then we shape our lives from those beliefs without thinking much about it. And by the time you were in your early twenties you developed some beliefs of your own, didn't you? The question is, did you stop there or have you continued to examine and question your beliefs?

As an adult, it's your responsibility to **stop and think about what you think**. No one can do it for you and no one can stop you from doing it. Think of your beliefs as filters everything passes through. If you see more problems and challenges than you do opportunities for growth, it's time to change the filters you view yourself, others and circumstances through.

What filters am I referring to? There are too many to mention, but I will point out two:

- The *This Is Good* filter
- The *This Is Bad* filter

When something happens, most people put it through their *This Is Good* or their *This Is Bad* filter. Then they feel either "good" or "bad" as a result. For instance, someone gets fired and he or she automatically puts it through the *This Is Bad* filter. What if he or she learned to filter the challenge through the *This Is Good* filter? Or what if he or she added a filter named *What If This Is a Good Thing?* That filter would at least allow for the possibility something good could come from what seems like a "bad" situation at the time.

Think about something in your life you wish you could change right now. What if you asked yourself what lessons you could learn from it or how you could grow from the experience—before anything changed? After all, if you're going to go through something "bad" you might as well get something good from it.

What if you believed you can't move forward in life until you learn the lessons to be learned from your current situation? Would that make you think before you automatically put something through the *This Is Bad* filter? Would that help you to stop and ask "What is the opportunity for me to learn and grow here?"

Coaching Assignment: Take a minute and list three things you've been putting through your *This Is Bad* filter (Something from your past or something going on in your life now.)

1. _____

2. _____

3. _____

Most people would think it absurd or harsh of you to suggest that something they consider to be "Bad" is only bad because they declare it to be so. However, how many times have you thought something was "Bad" in your life only to discover the good in it later?

I know what I'm talking about can be challenging to do, which explains why so few do it. Most people take the easier path, which makes for a more difficult life in the long run. You can do better than that and it starts with being conscious when you label something as "bad," "terrible" or as a "problem."

For instance, if you failed to get the promotion you wanted, would you automatically put it through your *This Is Bad* filter? Is not getting the promotion you wanted a bad thing? Most people would say "Of course it's a bad thing." But not everyone would agree. Most would, but not everyone.

A few would say it's a "good" thing for one reason or another. What if we viewed a challenge we're facing through the perspective Joseph Campbell offers:

> **"Where you stumble, there your treasure lies."**

What if our default response to a setback was, "What is the lesson I can learn from this?" or "How can I view this in a way that will allow me to re-envision my life and re-invent myself?"

When you look at a problem, do you assume *there are solutions* at hand? Or do you believe things will stay the same or get worse? How do you know that? You don't. So why treat your assumptions, perspectives and beliefs as facts? When I was a teenager, I read Napoleon Hill's book *Think and Grow Rich* and added (and nurtured) a new belief into my subconscious mind:

> **"In every adversity, there is the seed of an equivalent or greater benefit."**

There have been times in my life where I have doubted that perspective, struggled with it and even forgotten it. But it always came back to me. I understand that if you're going through difficult times, the belief that every adversity contains a seed of an equal or greater benefit might frustrate you or even "make you angry."

That's okay. I don't take that statement literally—I take it as a principle in life and use it the best I can. It's not that every adversity is made good just because there's a benefit to be gained from it. For instance, having a child born with serious health problems isn't something any parent would ever want.

The point is if something is heart-wrenching, we don't have to make it worse than it is. We want to acknowledge the pain and at the same time to actively learn, grow and transform from it.

If a parent of a sick child learns to be more compassionate or learns to value what is more important in life, that doesn't turn the storm in their life into blue skies. However, it does allow them to temper their pain with what they take away from their experience.

This is more empowering than the alternative. You *could* choose to be cynical, to be angry and to lash out at life and at others or to give up. That can be tempting at times and it would even seem to make perfect sense at times.

However, consider that whatever perspective you live from is going to come back to you in some way and on some level. With that in mind, do your best to bring the most useful perspective you can to any challenge or tragedy that you have experienced. Do the same with the opportunities that come your way so you can make the most of them.

It's healthy to question what we believe and to test our beliefs to see if a change might be in order—even if it can be scary at times. If a belief isn't taking you where you want to go or making you feel the way you want to feel at any given time, would it make sense to rethink it? After all, **what's a belief good for if it's not good for you?**

Why not live your life from the most useful, powerful and empowering beliefs you can discover and build into your belief system? Why do that? Because your perspective, your belief(s) at any given moment can:

- Frame your situation as a "problem"
- Make your problems seem bigger than they are
- Blind you to solutions at hand
- Keep you from taking action
- Make you forget how powerful and capable you are

On the other hand, your perspective can:

- Frame your situation as an opportunity to learn, grow and transform
- Shrink your problems down to size
- Open your eyes to solutions
- Move you into action
- Make it easier to tap into your powerful self and take action

The perspective we take and the stories we tell ourselves explain why some of us feel overwhelmed or defeated by our challenges and some of us feel energized and motivated by them. In his book *Learned Optimism*, Martin Seligman, Ph.D. describes the stories we tell ourselves as *explanatory styles*.

Seligman tells us pessimists and optimists operate from distinctly different beliefs and perspectives when they look at themselves and their challenges. Seligman notes that pessimists view their mistakes, setbacks and failures as:

- **Personal:** "This is my fault—I don't have what it takes" versus "I didn't have the tools I needed to succeed with this before, but I can get them now."

- **Pervasive:** "I fail at everything important to me" versus "I failed with this one thing."

- **Permanent:** "This will never change" versus "This is temporary and I can change it."

What if you developed the mindset—the beliefs—that instead of thinking *you* were the problem, it was simply a matter of learning the skills you needed for more happiness or success? What if you believed that any one failure was just that—one failure? What if you believed your mistakes, setbacks and any one failure—or string of failures—were temporary, not permanent?

Can you see and feel how those beliefs would enable you to bounce back from any setback and propel you forward? Decide today to learn and nurture the beliefs and perspectives in life that will create the happiness, health and abundance you deserve. I call these types of beliefs "useful" beliefs. The question is, how do you to determine if any given belief is useful to you or not?

You determine the usefulness of a belief or perspective by the results it produces. Here is the litmus test for a useful belief: **Does it give you positive energy that fuels taking effective action?** For instance, notice the difference between thinking "I can't do this" versus "This is challenging and it might take me some time, but it's possible."

Here's how William Arthur Ward puts it: "The pessimist complains about the wind; the optimist expects it to change; the realist adjusts the sails." Each person, the pessimist, the optimist and the realist has their own perspective. I add a fourth category to this mix: The *optimistic realist*. That way we can acknowledge *what is* while expecting things to change as we "adjust the sails" for any given circumstance.

Recently, I coached five of my clients to find jobs that gave them more responsibility, opportunity and income than their previous positions. Interestingly enough, they weren't thinking of seeking other opportunities as we began the coaching. However, when I asked each of them if they wanted more fulfilling and rewarding work, instead of saying, "Yes," each one of them responded with their "reasons" (beliefs) as to why they couldn't find a much better job.

One client believed his lack of a college degree kept him from getting a better job. Another client told me "There are only a small number of companies in my industry" and "My $350,000 salary would be almost impossible to replace and I've waited too long to make a change."

Both clients were making the mistake of thinking the past determines what's possible for the present or the future. You've likely heard the statement, "The past doesn't equal the future." Most of us believe that on a conscious level and that's good. However, when you believe that on the deeper subconscious level, you will create incredible change in your life.

The fact is no matter what has happened or what your situation is or whether you judge it to be "good" or "bad"—you have the power to dramatically change your view of things. Carl Jung, M.D. said, "I am not what happened to me, I am what I choose to become."

The first book I read as a teenager was a small volume titled *Your Greatest Power* by J. Martin Kohe. It began to shape my beliefs about life being an adventure and a journey with unlimited possibilities.

I was curious as to what the author would say our greatest power was. I found out he believed it to be our ability to determine the choices we make. I learned that we could grow our self-awareness and we could change the perspective we bring to any circumstance we face in life.

That was heady stuff for a teenager, but I took it in the best I could. It wasn't until many years later though that I began to really learn to choose my thoughts and beliefs and to change my life. I began to realize just because we "know" something doesn't mean we "get it."

Sometimes we have to experience setbacks, disappointments and failures to come back to what we thought we knew and learn it for the first time.

The most important thing isn't what happens to us, it's the attitude we bring to it and to our life overall. Despite our challenges and setbacks, we can develop a mindset of abundance and positive expectancy. When we do that, we are confident and bold in what we ask of ourselves and what we ask from life.

Shortly after reading the book mentioned above I came across another book with a thought provoking poem:

I Bargained With Life

*"I bargained with Life for a penny,
And Life would pay no more,
However I begged at evening
When I counted my scanty store;*

*For Life is a just employer,
He gives you what you ask,
But once you have set the wages,
Why, you must bear the task.*

*I worked for a menial's hire,
Only to learn, dismayed,
That any wage I had asked of Life,
Life would have paid."*

- Jesse B. Rittenhouse

Rittenhouse tells us life is like a mirror that reflects back to us our subconscious thoughts, beliefs and expectations and actions—our level of consciousness. Life gives back to us what we believe and therefore *expect* to receive from it. The question is, "What do you expect from Life—success and happiness or difficulty and frustration?

Albert Einstein stated, "I think the most important question facing humanity is, "Is the universe a friendly place?" Do you believe the "Universe," "Life," or "God" wants you to succeed, to be happy and fulfilled in life?

The late Clement Stone talked about being an *Inverse Paranoid*. A paranoid person believes someone or everyone is "against" them in some way and "out to get them." The *Inverse Paranoid* believes the universe and people are conspiring for his or her good. Some think that's ridiculous or even delusional—what do you think?

Who do you think is going to be in a better position to bring about the change they want? The person who believes the odds are stacked against them or the person who believes they live in a friendly universe and there are more than enough people willing to help them succeed?

I know from personal experience there are people ready to take advantage of us or even seriously harm us. I also know there are people who can be trusted and who will be in our corner. We need to be aware of the first group and we need to expect, look for and build relationships with second group.

You have to decide what you believe about life, people, your worth and your capabilities. That's because you need to have useful and empowering beliefs for the challenging times in life. It's easy to be courageous, imaginative and purposeful when you think things are going your way.

What about when you feel like things are out of control and falling apart? What about when you are burned out? When you're struggling in some way, that's when you need to know you have the power inside you to assert yourself and to create what you want and deserve.

> **"In the depth of winter I finally realized that there was in me an invincible summer." – Albert**

You need to know that you will not just survive your challenge; you will discover reservoirs of strength and resiliency you didn't know you had. You can rediscover your powerful self and take charge of your circumstances and life. That mindset will take you from treading water to walking on water. How would that feel?

Most people know about Post Traumatic Stress Disorder (PTSD). But have you ever heard of PTG—Post Traumatic Growth? Not many have. It's a term coined by Richard Tedeschi, Ph.D. and Lawrence Calhoun, Ph.D in 1995. Post Traumatic Growth suggests that even trauma can be a catalyst for personal growth and transformation.

How you view stress or trauma has consequences. There is evidence that suggests if you think stressful events or situations in your life will damage your health that belief is what you really need to be concerned about, more than what has happened to you. The bottom line is your beliefs and your stories about the stress in your life will affect the amount of stress you feel and the impact it has on you.

The question then is, "How do you view your challenges, especially your biggest ones? Do you believe you can not only handle them but learn and grow from them? **The fact is there is more to you than you think and you are more than you can imagine. You were born with the instinct to thrive and you are capable of learning how to do that even in the midst of great challenges.**

If you need help to see that, you're in good company. One reason why athletes and elite professionals have coaches is they know someone on the outside can help them gain perspective and achieve greater things than they could on their own. And isn't that what we learn from the story of Helen Keller?

When you feel challenged, you can go inside and listen to that aspect of self always connected to the source of *Positive Energy*—whatever you think that is. Even when you feel you can't go any further, you have more inside you than you realize.

Too often we get hypnotized by our challenges and we end up feeling our challenges are bigger and more powerful than we are. They're not, but if we perceive them to be, for all practical purposes, they will be.

What if we lived from the deep belief that we have a force of infinite energy inside that is more powerful, creative and positive than anything that happens on the outside? What if we listened to our intuition telling us there are always solutions, there are always people who want to support our dreams and efforts and that we are the creative force in our life?

What if we believed that we have within us all the resources we need to bounce back from any challenge or setback and we have a source of creative energy to propel us forward, no matter what? What if we believed our challenges were opportunities to learn from and to realize and embrace more of who we are and what we are truly capable of being and achieving?

Even if you said you don't believe that right now—wouldn't entertaining that belief be more useful than believing you couldn't meet whatever challenges you face?

Why don't we question our less than useful beliefs and perspectives more often? Simply because we haven't learned how to do that yet. When we're in the middle of a difficulty, **we think our perspective is reality, so we don't question it.** That's what keeps us stuck at times. The key to moving forward is to question your belief or perspective and test another one out.

If you don't question your current beliefs, you will continue to live your life from them. If you continue to live your life from the beliefs you have had up until now you will continue to experience the same results you've experienced. It doesn't get any simpler than that.

Coaching Assignment: (Sign your name and put the date of your commitment on the line below.)

"I commit to examining and questioning the beliefs I

bring to every situation in life.

Name: Date:

Jack, a former client, called me one day to re-engage me as his coach because his life had changed dramatically and suddenly. He was the C.E.O. of a company, had power, influence, a large salary and traveled internationally for business and pleasure. Then one day, two board members swayed the other board members and let Jack know his days were numbered.

He came into my office angry and afraid and asked me, "How could they do this to me, after all these years?" The first two months were incredibly hard for Jack—he had to come to terms with losing his job and he had to face having his "power" stripped from him. Jack soon realized his title and the perks that came with it were only an illusion of power; his *real power was within him, not outside of him*.

Jack's new insights enabled him to take charge of his fears, challenges and opportunities. He learned that there is always a gap, however small, between what happens to us and how we respond to it. Within that gap is our power to choose our perspective, our choices and our actions:

As Dr. Frankl put it:

"Between stimulus and response there is a space. In that space is our power to choose our response. In our response lies our growth and freedom."

Jack decided to reinvent himself and redesign his life. He allowed me to help him develop deeper trust in himself. That trust allowed him to step outside his comfort zone and to unleash more of his potential. Jack learned what most people don't understand—the quickest way to change your outer circumstances is to change your perspective.

As Wayne Dyer, Ph.D. wrote, "If you change the way you look at things, the things you look at change."

You can't control everything that happens in what we call the outer universe—if you can, please give me a call. What you can "control" is what happens in your inner universe. If you want to transform yourself and your life, you have to start with your beliefs and perspectives. Like it or not, you are the deciding factor in whether you feel powerless or powerful, hesitant or determined, held back or ready to take off and fly.

If that is so, let me ask you this question again: Why don't we change our beliefs and perspectives more often?

Because...

- We *assume* a particular belief is true—after all, "If it wasn't true, I wouldn't have believed it in the first place."
- We are often biased against any new beliefs that conflict with our current beliefs. In the world of psychology, we call this *Confirmation Bias* and we're usually not aware of it.

We have beliefs for *every* area and aspect of our lives—and we spend a lot of time and energy confirming, protecting and defending our beliefs. In fact, many of us argue for the very beliefs that limit us. For instance, we tell ourselves and others why we can't make more money, "lose weight" or find a better job in a "bad" economy.

The fact is how you look at any situation in your life either motivates you or discourages you. Here's how John Milton put it:

> **"The mind is its own place and in itself can make a Heaven of Hell, a Hell of Heaven."**

Milton's observation is lost on most of us. The fact is too many of us give our circumstances far more power than we give the incredible creative force of energy within us. Please know I'm not talking about something esoteric here.

Working on the quality of your thoughts, beliefs and perspective is as practical as it gets.

Here's my coaching challenge to you: **Don't believe your beliefs.** Don't treat them as facts. Recognize your beliefs for what they are—your opinion on the matter. How many things have you believed in the past that you no longer do? Growing up, did you believe in Santa Claus, the Easter Bunny or the Tooth Fairy? Did you believe at one time your parents knew everything and could do anything? At the time, all those beliefs seemed to be facts of life.

That's how we make change hard for ourselves. We think how we view our situation or how we see ourselves is "the way it is." It's not the way it is—it's the way we see it. **Unless you're infallible, that means everything you think regarding yourself, your capabilities, or your challenges is simply your opinion.**

I understand there are some facts involved with every event and circumstance in life. If your credit cards are maxed out or if you just lost your job, those are facts. However, what you tell yourself about those facts is what I'm addressing. The facts in your life aren't what is most important. What you do with them is.

The story you make up from those facts and how that story shapes your "attitude" about yourself, your life and your circumstances is what's most important. As Victor Frankl, M.D. put it:

> **"The last of human freedoms is the ability to choose one's attitude in a given set of circumstances."**

In other words, *your "problem" isn't the problem.* **Most often, your problem is how you think about your problem.** The beliefs you bring to your "problem" will either dig your hole deeper or they will become the elevator you use to get out of your hole.

You can change any challenge in your life if you change how you view it and how you view yourself in relationship to it. I'm not saying doing that is easy—it's not for most people. However, you can learn how to do it until it gets easier. You can practice the art of seeing your challenges from different vantage points that give you leverage over them.

Let me tell you about Sandra. She came to me "running on fumes" and feeling burned out in her career. When I asked her what she wanted to do career-wise, she was hesitant to tell me. It turns out Sandra had always dreamed of being a professional speaker—and she thought there was no way that could happen.

I could relate to her because I've traveled North America speaking and training employees for both small and large companies and I know the difference I make. There was one workshop I will never forget. A participant came in an hour late and I could tell right away something was troubling him.

The workshop was on *Thriving Under Pressure* and an hour into the workshop "John" explained that he had been diagnosed with stomach cancer that morning. I asked him how he was able to come to my workshop after getting such news. He looked at me and said, "I'm here because I need your help."

Why did I tell you this story? To let you know I understood Sandra's dream to be a speaker and her desire to help others by doing what she loved. After working together for three months, I filmed Sandra giving a fifteen minute presentation and she sent it to a company that hired speakers and trainers. Three months later she was hired.

Maybe you're like Sandra was and you don't think you can do work that's fulfilling and rewarding. However, just because you think you can't doesn't make it so. But if that's what you believe, it will be so for you—it will be your reality. But what is "reality"? Truth be told, what we call our "reality" is merely our *perception* of reality. When we say "The reality of this situation is…" what we really mean is, "This is how I see it."

How we see things is not reality—**it's merely our hallucination of what we call reality**. The fact is we hallucinate all the time. We have Negative Hallucinations—*failing to see* solutions around us or not seeing positive qualities in ourselves or others and so on. We also have Positive Hallucinations—seeing things that aren't really there—such as limitations and obstacles that aren't real.

Coaching Challenge: *Practice hallucinating what you want, not what you don't want—imagine being who you want to be and imagine having what you want in your life.*

Most people do the opposite. When they're faced with a challenge, their automatic response is to worry, hesitate and to imagine (hallucinate) things staying the same or getting worse. What do you think most people's automatic response is when they get called into their boss's office? Unless everything is going really well, they hallucinate all the things that could be a problem.

I'm sure you've heard a friend or colleague talk about having to give a presentation at work saying, "I have to make a presentation at work and just the thought of that freaks me out." What are they doing? They're hallucinating how stressful it's going to be and they're using their imagination (hallucinating) to predict a bad experience.

Your mind is a powerful tool and you can use it to make life easier or more difficult for you. When you think about your future (tomorrow, next week or next year) why not hallucinate things the way you want them to be? Why not imagine the happiness, success and outrageous good fortune you deserve?

With that said, let me say this again: If you're facing some challenges in a relationship, in your career or with your health, be honest with yourself about how you feel about your challenges. We don't make things better by saying "I'm fine," and we don't have to be embarrassed or ashamed when we're feeling overwhelmed or devastated.

Coaching Assignment: Be honest about how you feel

at any given moment—but build in times where you think and imagine things getting better.

Now let's talk about how our perspectives and beliefs can make our challenges more difficult than they have to be. Here are three ways we do that:

- **Distortions** — Distorting the facts and evidence: "I have the worst boss ever," or "I've done *everything* I can."
- **Deletions** — Deleting facts and evidence: "I'm not successful" Really? Not on any level or in any area of your life? When we delete information, we distort the overall facts and end up drawing conclusions based upon incomplete information.
- **Generalizations** — Generalizing from specifics: "I failed to reach my goal" becomes "I usually fail, so why should this time be different?" Here's another popular generalization: "Life is hard." Hard for whom? In what way is life hard? Is life hard all the time?

Our beliefs and thinking patterns make it easier or more difficult to deal with a given circumstance or to take advantage of an opportunity. We can either learn to think from an empowered and enlightened perspective or we can let our brain and subconscious mind run on autopilot and create fear, hesitation and a victim mindset.

The next time you are in a less than useful mood or frame of mind, stop and realize you're letting your mind run on autopilot. You're simply playing old mental scripts and beliefs you've learned in the past. Realize that when you're playing those old scripts, *you're hallucinating* and giving yourself less than useful hypnotic suggestions along the way.

Coaching Assignment: When you find yourself

letting your mind run on autopilot in a less than useful way, stop and remind yourself you can interrupt your "trance" and shift into a different trance that taps into your power to think and feel like the strong, capable and worthy person you are.

I cannot overemphasize the need for you to exercise patience and empathy with yourself as you are learning and practicing these new beliefs and behaviors.

Many intelligent, talented and capable people get hijacked by their emotions as they seek to change their lives. They allow their circumstances to push a button and trigger old mental scripts and mental movies and they let things run on autopilot.

They get hypnotized by their circumstances into believing that they aren't the creative force of energy in their life. However, you know that your circumstances don't control your happiness, confidence and peace of mind.

Your state of happiness doesn't depend upon *your state of circumstance*. We know this to be true because some people are unhappy in the best of circumstances and some people are happy even in the "worst" of circumstances. How do you explain that?

The answer lies in their perspective—how they view their situation.

How can someone be "happy" in the middle of hard times or even tragedy? Remember my definition of enlightened happiness? It's *feeling positive energy about yourself and your life, or feeling positive energy about the progress you're making.*

You can feel happy no matter what is going on around you by learning how to feel more competent and worthy about yourself in the moment and trusting yourself to handle what's going on. When you have the faith and confidence that you will get through the hard times, you'll naturally take the action you need to improve or change any circumstance you're in.

It's not that you won't struggle with doubts, fears or feel like you can't make it at times. No one feels at peace or powerful all the time—everyone has gone through a hard time or will sometime in the future.

However, the hard times are easier when you believe in yourself and know you will come out on the other end stronger, more resilient and with new perspectives in life.

If that's not your current mindset and you don't have the confidence you want, you can get it by building new beliefs and neural pathways in your brain.

Neuroscience tells us you can literally rewire your brain. The term for that is *neuroplasticity*.

In 1949, Canadian neuropsychologist Donald Hebb noted that **"Neurons that fire together, wire together."** That means the more you entertain beliefs and thoughts that embody confidence, the more they "wire" together to form stronger and more connected neurons.

Once neurons are wired together, they will grow stronger the more you use them—and the good news is your brain goes to the strongest neurons first. That's why I emphasize how important it is to consciously rewire your brain by thinking the new thoughts and beliefs you want *over and over again*—with *emotion*—until they are the dominant neurons in your brain.

Does that take effort on your part? Yes. Reading books, listening to audios, using effective affirmations, crafting vision boards, being around happy, confident and loving people, taking action and focusing on your strengths and the progress you make in life—all these things take some effort—but it's effort that will pay you back far more than you put in.

The key is to get started. If you want to change the way you think and *internalize* the thinking and the transformative energy in this book, read it five to ten times. You want to become so familiar with the content of this book that it begins to change your thinking, your self-talk and your automatic responses to what's going on around you.

Remember, the first secret of *Enlightened Happiness* is ***Your*** **Beliefs Create *Your* Reality**. Decide today to keep rewiring your brain to make your life easier, happier and more fulfilling. For now, here are a few things to think about:

"Everything we know of today was first imagined—and then believed into reality." - Alan Allard

"Despite what might seem to be the saddest and most intractable situation, we have the power to believe that something else is possible, that things can change, that a miracle can happen."
- Marianne Williamson

"You'll see it when you believe it." - Wayne Dyer, Ph.D

"Each of us tends to think we see things as they are; that we are objective. But this is not the case. We see the world, not as it is, but as we are - or, as we are conditioned to see it."
- Stephen Covey, Ph.D.

"Belief creates the actual fact." *- William James*

SECRET TWO: YOUR INNER VISION IS THE MENTAL BLUEPRINT FOR YOUR FUTURE

"If you limit your choices only to what seems possible or reasonable, you disconnect yourself from what you truly want, and all that is left is a compromise."
- Robert Fritz

"Your vision will become clear only when you can look into your own heart. Who looks outside, dreams; who looks inside, awakes."
- Carl Jung, M.D.

The second secret to *Enlightened Happiness* is **Your Inner Vision is the Mental Blueprint for Your Future.** Your Inner Vision is how you see your future unfolding, whether that's this week, next month or next year. Before we can arrive at a destination, we have to know what that destination is and why we want to go there.

Stephen R. Covey, Ph.D., author of *Seven Habits of Highly Successful People* puts it this way: "**Begin with the end in mind.**" To create something you have to be able to describe what that something is. If you already had the best life you could imagine, what would it look and feel like? Most people can't answer that question with clarity. They are so busy with day to day things they haven't taken the time to get clear about what their vision for their life is. However, here's the struggle most people have with imagining their ideal life—they limit themselves to far less than what they are capable and deserving of.

The vision most people have for their life is far more limited than they think. Designing your Life Vision is about getting clear on what matters most to you and what you are naturally drawn to and then continually testing the limits to see what is possible.

Did you see the quote by Robert Fritz at the top of this chapter? It's so good I'm going to repeat it:

> **"If you limit your choices only to what seems possible or reasonable, you disconnect yourself from what you truly want, and all that is left is a compromise."**

This is where most people sell themselves short. What do you *really* want and what are you *really* capable of? For most people, the answer is more than what their life is reflecting right now. Why is that?

It's because **few of us have had the guidance and the support we need** to get clear on who we are, what we want and what we can become and achieve. We are more powerful, capable and deserving than we know. In fact most people would say they are living lives below their true potential. Again, why is that?

One reason is we see those around us compromising what they really want for what they think is "reasonable." That's the environment we live in and environment has a powerful effect on us. Think about your early childhood environment and how it shaped your thinking and behaviors:

Were you taught to think big and to go for what is "impossible"? Did you learn to take risks and learn along the way? Or were you taught to play it safe? Did you learn to fear making mistakes or to dread failure? Whatever you've been doing in your life is what you learned to do somewhere along the way.

The fact is we were all taught and conditioned how to think and feel about ourselves, our capabilities, our needs and desires, our values and our dreams. **Were you taught that what you wanted was important and that you should be bold about asking for what you want?** Most of us weren't—we were taught the opposite. Children are taught, for the most part, to fit in, go along, and most important, to not rock the boat.

In school, we were taught to sit still, be quiet and to follow the rules. That conditioning continued when we got our first job. For the most part, leaders and managers want compliance and conformity. Leaders say they want creativity, innovation and disruption but how they react to these things says otherwise. They don't have the culture or the confidence that allows it, much less encourages it. So their employees go in and do the same thing, day in and day out, like the assembly line workers.

That might sound harsh, but it's reality for most organizations. Where is the fire and passion in our workplaces? The answer is there is some but it's not the norm. Childhood conditioning to play it safe is reinforced at work and in society at large.

No one told us the price we'd have to pay if we followed the crowd, suppressed our dreams and played it "safe." So we do work we might like but aren't passionate about, go home and get up the next day to do it all again. It's no wonder the Gallup Poll tells us only about thirty percent of us are engaged at work—meaning emotionally invested in our work and connected to those we do it with.

We can't condition people to fear mistakes and failure and then expect them to be fully engaged. We can't keep asking more of people while giving them less and then expect the full measure of their genius. And we can't fire employees "at will" when the company goes through rocky financial times and then expect loyalty in return. But that's what we're used to so we settle for what is and lose any vision of something exceptional.

Think about how your past programming has affected your happiness and your ability to not just survive in life and at work, but to thrive. Of course, in some ways your past conditioning has programmed you for happiness and success. Yet, in other ways, you were conditioned to doubt yourself, to hold back and to play a role much smaller than you are designed to play.

Don't you think life has more to offer you than you've discovered so far? Is it possible that who you think you should be and what you think you are capable of pales in comparison to what you could be and what you could achieve in life?

Think about what Eldon Taylor, Ph.D. wrote:

> **"I urge you to think back to who you were before you were told who you should be."**

Stop and ask yourself this question, "Can I expect anything in my life to change for the better if I don't change the Inner Vision my subconscious mind has to work with?" Is it time to update your Inner Vision to reflect what you **really** want your life to be like? *Is it even time to be audacious?*

After all, we really don't know what our limits are, do we? However, the problem isn't our limitations; the problem is *our illusion of how we're limited.* The only way to know what your limitations are is to go to the edge and test them. It's not likely that what you have thought to be your limitations are your real limitations.

I'm not saying we're not limited in *any* way. If you're

sixty-five years old and want to be a pro basketball player, I wish you the best. I won't put my money on that bet though. However, if you identify the things you *can* do that come from purpose, inspiration and love, you will be amazed at what is possible.

One thing that keeps us from thinking bigger, or from rediscovering our buried dreams, is we think what we want on deeper levels is beyond our reach or that it would demand too much of us. How have you limited yourself because you prematurely decided something was out of your reach? Think about that one.

How often do you begin to think about what you really want and then doubts, insecurities and fears pop up? Or, perhaps you begin to think big and those around you look at you like you're crazy. Before you know it, you're thinking about the obstacles and all the reasons you can't change or achieve what you want. And when you focus on your obstacles and challenges, they will hypnotize you into surrendering.

Coaching Assignment: List three ways you have demonstrated "I can't" thinking: ("I can't lose weight," I can't change jobs now," "I can't be happier until…")

1. _____

2. _____

3. _____

Do you think to earn more money you have to work longer and harder? How do you know that's true? You don't, but that's how most people think. Even if you did work longer hours, if you loved what you were doing, would it really be work? What if least considered that life could be easier and more enjoyable than you thought? I know that's possible and so do many of my clients. Here's one example:

When Nora came to me, she was making over six figures, but she was burned out. Shortly after she ended her coaching with me, Nora was earning almost three hundred thousand dollars a year while working less hours. What she thought was crazy and impossible turned out to be quite possible once she got started and kept going.

Let me tell you about another client. Susan is a sales professional and she has had a difficult past six months. She was barely paying her bills, and she couldn't see how things were going to get better. I knew what she was going through because I've certainly been there myself.

I often told Susan, "Your outer circumstances will change 'out of the blue' if you keep your mind on what you want." So she did that—with lapses along the way—but she focused on what she wanted enough to give her success a chance. A month later, she called me and told me her boss had accepted an offer from another company and wanted to take her with him.

Her new position came with a much higher salary and a better sales commission structure that will at least double her income. Also, Susan's new manager gave her two national accounts to manage that will bring her more money than she made the year before—and that doesn't factor in her additional sales beyond the national accounts.

What if Susan had failed to do the work of writing out a *Life Vision Statement* (you'll learn how to do this later in this chapter) and failed to keep going over it until her subconscious mind bought into it?

Let me tell you about another client—Patricia. She came into her first coaching session with great clarity of what she *didn't* want her life to be like. Patricia and her husband had been fighting and she was tired of that.

She also complained of how her body looked and she was dreading her upcoming tenth year college reunion. I asked Patricia if she realized that by giving her attention and energy to what she doesn't want, she was unintentionally telling her subconscious mind to create just that. Patricia *did* understand that—but she didn't know how stop doing it. She's not alone.

The truth is, your brain or your subconscious mind doesn't know how to *stop* doing anything—it only knows how to *start* doing something else. The only way to stop focusing on what you don't want is to **start focusing on what you do want.** Isn't that how meditating works? When your mind wanders, which it will often do—you simply bring it back to what you want to focus on.

Your job is to consciously put your attention on what you want and keep bringing your attention back to it, again and again. That's where a clear and compelling *Life Vision Statement* comes in. It will remind you again and again where you are going, what's important to you and what you want to create more of in your life.

Your *Life Vision Statement* is a document designed to keep your mind off of what you don't want **by keeping it on what you do want**. One way to do that is to read at least a small portion of your *Life Vision Statement* every day to seed your subconscious mind and to unleash the positive energy you need to create and manifest the life you want and deserve.

I know you want more for your life—but what *exactly* do you want? You simply cannot create or attract what you haven't yet clearly identified. An exceptional life demands clarity. Life is asking you this very moment, "What do you want?" How do you answer that question? Saying "I want my dream car" won't cut it. You have to put in a specific order for the specific car you want.

Once you are clear on what you want, you need to keep envisioning it until it becomes your dominant thinking. Your subconscious mind needs clarity. Think of your subconscious mind as an architect. You wouldn't tell your architect "I want a beautiful house that's perfect for my family." If that's all you told your architect, he or she wouldn't even know where to begin.

We often give our subconscious mind the details of what we **don't** want—and that's what your "architect" thinks you want it to build. We do that when we mentally replay something unpleasant from the past or when we worry about something happening in the future. When we do that, our subconscious mind thinks that's what we want. *Your dominant thoughts are the blueprint for your subconscious mind.*

That's why the late Earl Nightingale taught "You become what you think about." And Lillian Whiting stated "The vision always precedes the reality." If you want something to change in your life, you have to change your mental blueprint—and not just on the conscious level—but on the subconscious level as well.

If you've tried to change or improve something in your life or tried to reach a goal you said was important to you, but failed, here are seven reasons why:

- **You're not clear on what you want:** "I know I want to do bigger and more meaningful things, but I'm not sure what that would be."

- **You have conflicting desires** that take you in different directions: "I want to make more money and to have a fuller life, but it seems like it would take too much work."

- **Fear:** Most people "deal" with their fear by ignoring it. They distract themselves in various ways so they don't have to think about their fear. The result is their fear keeps them from creating what they want.

- **You lack confidence:** You don't believe what you want is possible or "realistic." "I've done well for myself and I want to do something extraordinary, but what if I don't have what it takes? Do I really want to find out the answer to that question?"

- **You don't believe you are worthy of what you want:** This affects more people than you can imagine and is often the hidden barrier that keeps you from knowing what you want or keeps you from allowing it into your life.

- **You lack a skill you need to turn your inner vision into outer reality:** You want to start your own business or become an executive in your company but you haven't mastered the basics yet.

- **You don't have the support you need:** One reason coaching is so powerful is it gives you support you won't get elsewhere. That includes positive feedback but it also means challenging you. This is especially important for leaders at work because few leaders have someone who is willing to rock the boat and tell them what no one else will

These six factors keep you from feeling as competent, powerful and energized in life as you can be. They can also make it harder for you to write out your Life Vision, committing it to paper. For instance, you might not be clear on what your dream job would be, so you don't know what to write down. The solution to that is to begin where you are and write out what you do know.

I was talking with an executive recently about her difficulty in writing out her vision for where she wanted to take her team. What was important to her? Why did she go to work and what really moved her? She had a high performing team, but we both knew they could do even better and be more fulfilled.

At one point in the conversation I told her, "I think you're hesitating on getting clear on your vision because what you really dream about scares you and you don't think it's reasonable." She agreed, but there was more. You see, sometimes we're afraid of failure, but just as often we're afraid of success, as strange as that might sound.

Consider what Marianne Williamson says in *A Return From Love*:

"Our deepest fear is not that we are inadequate. Our deepest fear is that we are powerful beyond measure. It is our light, not our darkness that most frightens us. We ask ourselves, 'Who am I to be brilliant, gorgeous, talented, fabulous?' Actually, who are you not to be..."

"Your playing small does not serve the world. There is nothing enlightened about shrinking so that other people won't feel insecure around you. We are all meant to shine, as children do. We were born to make manifest the glory of God that is within us."

"It's not just in some of us; it's in everyone. And as we let our own light shine, we unconsciously give other people permission to do the same. As we are liberated from our own fear, our presence automatically liberates others."

Everyone struggles with fear on some level. The antidote to fear is to continue to nurture your self-worth and self-confidence. In the meantime, be honest about what your vision for you life is now and what you've been creating from it. Sometimes a client will tell me, "I have a vision for an incredible life—but that's not the kind of life I have right now."

When I say your life reflects your inner vision, I'm talking about the inner vision of your subconscious mind, not what you just envision with your conscious mind. The two have to be in agreement.

If you've been working on your vision and nurturing it consistently, then it's a matter of giving your subconscious mind more time to accept it. If you say "I want a job I love," or "I want to be happier," you have to do the work to influence your subconscious mind to embrace that.

Look at your outer circumstances—your results tell you what vision you've had (subconsciously) for yourself and your life. Perhaps you're familiar with the statements "As within, so without," and "As above, so below." If we want our outer circumstances to change, we need to work on our inner circumstances and craft a vision that inspires and moves us into action.

The reason is that life works from the inside out. Our inner thoughts and beliefs are like seeds planted in the ground. What lies underneath is what will show up on the outside. Lilian Whiting's statement is true: "The vision always precedes the reality."

If you want to see your outer circumstances in life change and improve you have to work from the inside out. As was discussed earlier, you can't directly change your circumstances. You have to indirectly change them by changing your thoughts, beliefs and behaviors.

Before your bank account can grow you have to grow your ability to see yourself as capable and worthy of earning more money. Before others start treating you with more respect, you have to give yourself more respect.

When your inner conditions improve, your outer conditions will improve.

This is hard for many people to wrap their minds around—especially their subconscious mind. They think they believe the statement above, but most don't. I know that because few people (comparatively speaking) invest their time and attention on a daily basis to improving their inner condition. The urgent crowds out the important.

If you want to transform yourself and your life, you have to make it a priority to do so. That means investing time and money—so start where you can with what you have.

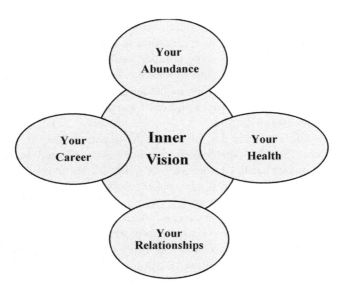

Tracy came to me upset that she was forty pounds overweight and told me she had tried every diet she knew of and had even hired a personal trainer. What she hadn't tried—or didn't know how to do yet—was to learn to love, accept and affirm herself. The more Tracy learned to feel good about herself, the less she used emotional eating to make herself feel better—and her body naturally shifted to a healthy weight.

Let's talk about your vision and an area many would like to improve, but struggle with believing they can—significantly increasing their income. If I asked most clients, "Can you double your income?" their automatic response would be "No." What about you? And do you realize your ability to create more money in your life is determined by *what you believe you're worth* and *what you believe you are capable of?*

You might be quite happy with your income and your life overall. You know you could earn more money but don't feel the desire to do so. However, that's not where most people are. Where are you in terms of how happy you are with your financial life? How do you limit yourself when it comes to financial abundance?

Think about J.K. Rowling of Harry Potter fame. She was on government assistance when she wrote her first book. A few years back, I was in a little café called *The Elephant House* in Edinburgh, Scotland with my wife where Rowling wrote some of her first book. When she first began to write, I doubt she envisioned the empire she would eventually build.

But Rowling had a dream and she began to write. You can do the same; *start where you are and see where it takes you.* Are you living from inspiration and joy? Are you surrounded by close friends and family who "get" you; and you them? Are you enjoying not only financial abundance but prosperity in all areas of life?

You can be and have all those things. The key is to start where you are with what you have. Never let what you can't do stop you from doing what you can do. Wherever you are now, you can start by creating a more compelling Inner Life Vision, one that describes a more fulfilling and rewarding life than what you are living now. Why is this so important? Whatever inner vision you've had, *that's what your subconscious mind thinks you want.* It's time to give your subconscious mind a vision worthy of the real you.

Julie, a client of mine long ago, had a great job but was unhappy because she was single and wanted to be married. She had been divorced for three years and I asked her, "What pops up in your mind when I ask you to think about yourself?"

Julie didn't skip a beat and replied, "I'm damaged goods because I'm divorced." I suggested to Julie that she think of herself as a single woman that any man would be lucky to have. She liked that. When she changed her inner vision of how she thought about herself and did some other inner work, her life changed. She met a great guy and today they have four wonderful children together.

What do you **really** want for yourself and your life?

Does your subconscious know what you really want or has it been confused by mixed messages? You already know on a subconscious level what you *really* want to achieve, to be and to experience in life. However, you might need to learn how to create a **safe inner environment** for it to surface to your conscious awareness.

Otherwise, your deeper desires will stay buried beneath your hurts, your disappointments and your fears. In my coaching, I help my clients to feel safe and to trust themselves on deeper levels. To have the life you want, you have to trust yourself. That's easier said than done, but you can always learn to trust yourself more. That increased trust will allow you to uncover your hidden desires, motivations and passions and tap into the creative force within you.

The truth is, it takes courage to be honest about what we really want—because we've learned to fear mistakes, disappointments and failures. If you want to be happier, you have to learn how to nurture your ability to love and accept yourself no matter what. When you do that, amazing things will happen.

Actor Jim Carrey tells the story of writing himself a *ten million dollar* check "for acting services rendered" and putting it in his wallet to regularly look at it. He was earning a million dollars per movie by then and the thought of earning ten million dollars per movie was a stretch for him. However, by that time, Carrey had a lot of practice challenging himself and thinking audaciously. At age ten he sent his resume to the Carol Burnett show.

Carrey was putting into action the principle that there are always two creations—the mental creation comes first, then the physical manifestation follows. Carrey also knew he needed to gently influence his subconscious mind into accepting new levels of expectations. What about you?

Your *Life Vision Statement* will help you to gently influence your subconscious mind. To get clear on what you want in your life, begin to write out what your ideal life would look like. Start with a rough draft of bullet point statements first.

Write fast and don't edit anything along the way; just get it down. Suspend your judgment about what is "possible," "realistic" or "right." When your subconscious gives you something, just let it flow onto the paper without judgment.

You can give more thought to what comes out later. If the thought of owning and flying a helicopter comes up for you, write that down. Your conscious mind might tell you you're crazy and that's perfectly fine.

Hear what it says without judgment. If your subconscious says you want to be a rock star, write it down. These are important clues for your conscious mind and you want to respect that. Go with the flow and write down whatever pops up for you.

This isn't the time to think about *how* you will achieve something. It's time to listen to your Higher Self. Your Conditioned Self (the aspect of self that was programmed to think in terms of what you "should" do, "ought to do," "have to do," "must do," or "can't do," etc.) might tell you that you are "selfish" for wanting certain things or that what you want isn't realistic. It might tell you, "You can never have that; who do you think you are?"

For now, just *focus on getting clear on what you want, not how you will get it*. The *how* will be revealed along the way as you take inspired action. *Your job is to get clear on the what first, and allow the how to be revealed at a later time.*

Coaching Assignment: Write down two things you've not taken action on because you don't know how you could make it happen:

1. _____

2. _____

Coaching Tip: You can create a *Vision Board* using

words and images from magazines and by putting them on a poster board, displaying them on your refrigerator or in your home office or wherever you will see them often. This will be a coaching tool to help you visualize how your life would be if it was the best you can envision for now.

You can also make a digital vision board and you can also have *several* vision boards; one for your overall life and several that are focus on health, relationships or financial abundance.

Bonus Coaching Tip: Instead of choosing between writing out your *Life Vision Statement* or creating a Vision Board on poster boards or digitally, you can do both.

Your job is to give your powerful subconscious mind a clear and exciting vision to work from. Be like a child again, imaginative, fearless and free. Remember, you already have an inner vision; the question is, **"Does your inner vision do you justice?"**

Before I show you how to create your *Life Vision Statement*, let me give you a fast way to begin. Write down seven things you want to create in your life or seven things you already have but want more of. Be as specific as you can for now. Make your own template on your computer or tablet so you can use it daily.

"I Want" (Or "I want more of")

1. _____
2. _____
3. _____
4. _____
5. _____
6. _____

7. _____

Here are some examples of how to get started with your *Life Vision Statement:*

Step One: Possible Areas of Your Life to Include
- Health
- Relationships
- Career Success
- Financial Abundance (Savings and investments, dream house, dream car, clothing and accessories, art, philanthropy, etc.)
- Travel
- Self-Development
- Recreation-Hobbies

You can name this document anything you want, such as *My Ideal Life* or *My Life Rocks!* (Label your categories in a way that inspires you and add to or subtract from the categories above.)

Step Two: The "Bullet Point" Start

Choose a category to begin with and use pen and paper or your computer or tablet to brainstorm. Think in broad terms and begin to list what pops up in your mind. For instance, in the category of career, what comes to mind?

If you could wave a magic wand and do work that fed both your soul and your bank account, what might that be? If you can't answer the question with specifics, answer it in more general terms. Here are some examples:

- "I wake up each morning excited to do work that is meaningful, challenging and energizing,"
- "My company recognizes and rewards me on a

consistent basis."
- "The people I work with are talented, collaborative and fun to be around."
- "My work brings out the best in me."
- "I am self-employed and I'm creating wealth for myself and others while having the time of my life."

Write out bullet points for each section and build on it as you go. Your *Life Vision Statement* is a work in progress you will update as you learn more about what you want and what you are willing to go for.

Have fun, be imaginative and *be audacious*.

Step Three: Fill In the Details

After you have completed the bullet points for each area of your life, go back and write out more detailed descriptions as needed. Describe how your life would be if you were living fearlessly—fear(less)ly. You can begin with general descriptions and get more specific later—remember, this is an ongoing project. Also, make sure you write everything in the present tense.

For instance, in your "Health" category:

- Exercise: "I exercise 3-5 times a week and love it" (Also write out what you will be doing for exercise, at least for now.) "My friends, family and co-workers tell me I look great."
- Eating: "I love eating foods that are healthy; I crave foods that nourish my body and give me plenty of energy and a sense of well-being."
- Sleep: "I wake up refreshed and excited about the day ahead of me."

After describe your ideal life in specific terms, go back and make sure your descriptions are written in the **positive** (What you want, not what you don't want: "I am healthy" versus "I *don't* have headaches.")

More examples:

- "I have $200K in my retirement account." (Put in a number that makes sense for now...you will increase that number as you keep revising your *Life Vision Statement.*)
- "My blood pressure is ____."
- "I love driving my Bentley Coup. It is red with black interior." (Continue your description in vivid detail.)
- "I live in a 3,500 square feet house on a lake. It has three garages, a movie room..."
- "I have two close friends with whom I spend regular time."

You now have plenty to begin writing out your *Life Vision Statement* today. Remember, the second secret to *Enlightened Happiness* is **Your Inner Vision Is Your Mental Blueprint For Your Future.**

Here are some things to think about concerning how important your Life Vision is:

"Your Vision is the promise of what you shall one day be. Your Ideal is the prophecy of what you shall at last unveil." - James Allen

"Your imagination is your preview of life's coming attractions."
-Albert Einstein

"No one is less ready for tomorrow than the person who holds the most rigid beliefs about what tomorrow will contain." - *Watts Wacker, Jim Taylor and Howard Means*

ALAN ALLARD, Ph.D.

"The true sign of intelligence is not knowledge but imagination."
-Albert Einstein

"To know what you prefer, instead of humbly saying 'Amen' to what the world tells you to prefer, is to have kept your soul alive."
-Robert Louis Stevenson

"I dream for a living." *- Steven Spielberg*

SECRET THREE: MASTER YOUR SELF-TALK, MASTER YOUR LIFE

"Words are, of course, the most powerful drug used by mankind."
- Rudyard Kipling

"Your mother might have told you, 'If you don't have something nice to say, don't say it.' Now add to that, 'If it's not nice, don't say it to yourself—and if it is nice, be sure to say it to yourself.'"
- Victoria Moran

The third secret to *Enlightened Happiness* is **Master Your Self-Talk, Master Your Life.** Your self-talk is simply your ongoing thoughts, what we can call your inner dialogue. Why is your self-talk so important to co-creating the reality you want and unleashing your potential? Here's why:

Your self-talk leads to your emotions, your emotions lead to your decisions, your decisions lead to your behaviors and your behaviors lead to your results.

If you want to change the results you are creating, start with your self-talk.

I can't emphasize this enough. If you learn how to use your self-talk to empower yourself, you will feel the positive energy you need to take effective action—and that will lead to positive results in your life.

When you learn how to talk to yourself in a supportive, nurturing and empowering way, *everything in your life will change for the better.*

Here's an email from one of my clients that illustrate that:

Hi Alan – I just have to congratulate myself for a quick victory I just had…(in fact, as I was typing this, I wrote quick "little" victory, and I realized it's not little)…I was just working on a client's website when I came up against a frustrating challenge. I threw my head back and arms up in the air and exclaimed something along the lines of…"This kind of stuff drives me up a freakin' wall!"

Then, I thought to myself... "Really?" I then got out my notebook and wrote myself this affirmation…

"Dealing with this kind of stuff is typical for web

designers—even advanced and intelligent web designers such as myself. In fact, after having successfully dealt with many similar setbacks in the past, I have developed patience, perseverance and a tough skin that enables me to easily and almost effortlessly move forward and find solutions quickly. I can then move on and enjoy my work and day."

I actually found a quick solution that I wasn't expecting, which afforded me the time to write you this email…congratulating myself! Who is this new me? Hope you're having a great day!

-Steve Pederson www.pedersonwebdesign.com.

(By the way, Steve is my webmaster, an accomplished musician and songwriter and I highly recommend him.)

The email from Steve demonstrates that what you say to yourself throughout the day creates your reality. We can either create frustration and unhappiness or we can tap into our power and create confidence and happiness. Our self-talk comes from the beliefs deep in our subconscious mind and that's why we spent so much time talking about your beliefs.

However, your conscious mind also plays a vital role in your happiness, success and well-being. You have to use your conscious mind to pay attention to your self-talk in order to change it. When it comes to changing self-talk, I'm frequently asked how we can change what is typically called "limiting beliefs" or "negative beliefs."

I don't use the term "limiting beliefs" because all beliefs are limiting in some way and I don't refer to "negative beliefs" because those terms aren't useful. What is useful is being aware of your self-talk and replacing less than useful self-talk with useful self-talk.

To do that, you have to have a strong enough "why" to do the work to transform your self-talk, so let's address that. We know that how we communicate with *others* is not just important—it's critical. At the same time, most people fail to understand how powerful their self-talk is. If I asked you if it made any difference how a mom or dad talked to their five year old, you would tell me it makes all the difference in the world.

Dr. Stephen Covey said when he was growing up, he would sometimes wake up from sleeping to find his mother standing over him saying things like, "You're going to do great on your test tomorrow. You can do anything you put your mind to." How would you have liked to have been "programmed" to think that way?

The fact is most of us didn't get that consistent message growing up. We can't change that and we can't control what others say to us today, but we can control what we say to ourselves. After all, it's called *self-talk*.

How important is your self-talk? Your self-talk determines:

- What you *feel*—your emotional energy
- What you *do*—and how well you do it
- The results you create in your life and work

How much thought do you give to your thoughts?

How often do you pay attention to the quality of your thinking? **Most people don't think much about their thinking.** They are constantly thinking, yet they seldom think about what they are thinking. Then they're confused about why they feel confident at times and hesitant and fearful at other times.

How you talk to yourself explains why you take action on some things and procrastinate on others. The fact is, **you literally talk yourself *into* something or you talk yourself *out* of it.** Elite athletes know how important their self-talk is—that's why they have coaches to help them with the psychological and emotional aspects of winning.

> "Elite athletes know their inner game determines their outer game."

If you want to know why you feel motivated at some times and unmotivated at other times, the answer lies in your self-talk. I'm not saying that your self-talk is the only factor that drives your emotional states. If you're tired on a physical level, that will impact your emotional state. However, your self-talk then affects how you feel physically. If you go around thinking and saying "I'm tired," that thinking will make you more tired because your body is always listening to you.

Your thoughts are powerful and you can learn to use them in a powerful way to your advantage. They create your emotional states, what I call your *Inner Weather Patterns*. Talk to yourself in ways that create positive expectancy and the sun will be shining. Talk gloom and doom and the clouds will hide the sun and your *Inner Weather Pattern* will be dark and stormy. If you want to feel like the sun is out, you have to create that inner light and warmth with your self-talk.

You are the one that creates and sustains whatever *Inner Weather Pattern* is going on inside you. Your inner emotional weather will always reflect your thoughts and self-talk. In other words, how you feel is determined by how you talk to yourself in the moment.

Marilyn vos Savant had the highest IQ ever measured in any human being for many years in a row. Someone once asked her what the connection was between emotions and thoughts. She said, **"Feeling is what you get for thinking the way you do."**

Think about how often you criticize or judge yourself in some way. Do you do that often or seldom at all? *Most people criticize themselves far more than they are aware of—and often their self-criticism is subtle.* Even when they're aware of it, they seldom stop to think "This isn't helping me—it's time to do something different." That's because few people ever pay attention to their thinking.

I suggested to a client that he begin to affirm himself every day. He responded, "Wait a minute, are you telling me to tell myself things just to make myself feel good—even if I'm not feeling good about myself? I don't want to lie to myself." I replied, "Aren't you lying to yourself every time you criticize yourself or tell yourself you can't have an extraordinary life? You thought you were telling yourself the truth, but you weren't. You were lying to yourself—and you believed the lie."

Isn't it interesting how many of us believe the negative things we say to ourselves and doubt or outright reject the positive things we could say to ourselves?

Why is it that when we tell ourselves something positive and affirming about ourselves we feel as if we're lying or at least exaggerating the facts? Yet when we tell ourselves something negative, we think it's the truth—why is that? Because that's how we learned to think.

That's good to know because if you don't like the results you're getting, you can do something else. Stop now and ask yourself if you're ready to make a commitment to talk to yourself in a way that gives you the results you want. Whatever answer you get, it's important for you to know.

Metaphorically speaking, we all have a fire within us, a force of life energy. You'll either add fuel to that fire or you can pour water on it—depending upon how you talk to yourself throughout the day.

When you criticize yourself, put yourself down in small or big ways, or when you deflect praise and compliments from others by saying "It's not a big deal, anyone could have done it," what are you doing? *You are holding yourself back. You are trash-talking yourself without realizing it.* You're not doing that intentionally, but that's the end result.

Please realize that when you criticize yourself, you make it more difficult to trust yourself. The self-criticism, judgment, shame and fear that you've learned early on in life all chip away at your ability to trust yourself. The more you learn how to trust yourself the easier and more enjoyable life gets.

That's because every decision you make, every step you take, requires you to trust yourself. Learn to tune into and listen to your Higher Self, whatever you consider that to be. You have a source of knowledge and wisdom inside you to guide you, empower you and support you.

When you listen to your Higher Self, you will feel energized, confident and at peace with yourself and with what's going on around you. Your Higher Self knows how powerful you are and how deserving you are. That aspect of yourself knows the difference between your behavior and who you are. It knows you are responsible for your behavior, but you are not your behavior.

Why have so few of us mastered our self-talk? The biggest reason is we haven't been taught how to do so. We haven't been taught to pay attention to our self-talk. It's like a subliminal program running beneath our level of conscious awareness. My challenge to you is to start noticing when you're criticizing yourself, especially in subtle ways.

Mastering your self-talk requires your attention. It requires your commitment, patience and focus.

If you want to become aware of your self-talk, you have to choose to do so—*it won't happen on its own*. Choose one or two times a day to pay close attention to your inner dialogue by listening closely or by writing it down—even for three minutes or less. Perhaps the fastest way to transform you self-talk is to have a coach. He or she will hear things you say that don't register with you, give you feedback and accelerate you mastering your self-talk.

Brad was a client who learned to make his self-talk work for him. When he started coaching with me he had no idea how often he talked himself out of things he wanted in life. He would begin by talking about something he wanted to achieve, such as a promotion, and then he would begin to think of all the reasons it wouldn't happen.

Brad would say, "I'm in my fifties now and my company doesn't promote people my age." Then Brad would put himself down by saying, "I should have gone to college when I got out of the military—what was I doing with my life?" It's no wonder Brad often felt stuck and unmotivated.

Imagine how you would feel if someone followed you around, making negative comments, focusing on what you haven't yet achieved and talking from a place of lack and fear. How would that affect you over time?

Are you that person who follows yourself around making such comments?

Fortunately Brad decided to master his self-talk. He learned how to use enlightened self-talk and his self-confidence grew dramatically, his work improved and he eventually achieved the promotion he had wanted for so long. When he asked his boss why he wasn't promoted earlier, his boss told him, "You didn't have the confidence you needed then."

When you change your self-talk, you will be surprised at what happens internally and externally. Your outer circumstances will begin to change and align with what is going on inside you. Changing your self-talk is the beginning of changing your life.

Coaching Assignment: Rate your self-talk. Circle the number below to rate how empowering your overall self-talk is.

$$1 - 2 - 3 - 4 - 5 - 6 - 7 - 8 - 9 - 10$$

Think about your answer and how it matches up with how you're doing in major areas of your life. The more empowering your self-talk is, the higher quality results you produce in life.

One thing I often do in my workshops is to put people

in groups of three. I have two of them stand slightly behind one person, one on the right and one on the left. For sixty seconds, two people are talking while the person in front is listening. Listening to what?

To affirming statements such as: "You are smart, you can trust yourself, you are worthy of all the good things in life you want, you're a great listener, you are intelligent, you can do what you put your mind to."

By the time everyone has experienced listening to so many empowering statements, the room is buzzing with energy. Think about it. How many people hear those kinds of things throughout the day? Very few—because few of us talk to ourselves that way and few of us have others talking to us in such an affirming way.

Coaching Assignment: Start writing down some of your self-talk at least once a day to remind yourself how important and powerful it is. Write down something you are thinking in the moment about yourself, your life, your relationships or your health. Sometimes the self-talk you write down will be empowering and at other times it will be otherwise. Either way is fine. The key is to develop the habit of paying attention to your self-talk.

Begin to notice that how you talk to yourself creates your emotions in the moment and remind yourself that your emotions are the fuel that drives your performance. When you use empowering self-talk, you feel on top of the world. When you use disempowering self-talk, you feel the weight of the world. Noticing that is the start to improving your self-talk.

Start to discover that when you compliment yourself, you feel positive energy. And when you criticize yourself you drain yourself of that positive energy and create a less than useful energy.

Learn how to talk to yourself in a way that is consistent with whom you want to be and with what you want to achieve and experience in life. When you transform your self-talk, you will change how you feel about yourself, how you envision your future and how quickly you take action towards your goals.

The WYSTTYBF" Test:

What if you talked to yourself the way you talk to someone you respect and admire? How would your self-talk change? The next time you're feeling frustrated or unmotivated, stop and pay attention to your thoughts. What are you saying to yourself? Write down what you were saying to yourself and then ask yourself this question: **"Would You Say That to Your Best Friend?"**

I call it The *"WYSTTYBF" Test*. (Sounds "Wistibif") I guarantee that if all you do is use the *WYSTTYBF Test* for ninety days your life will change more than you can imagine. I know that's a strong statement so why not find out for yourself?

How do you talk to someone you love and respect? Would you tell them, "You *shouldn't* have made that mistake—you're better than that," or, "You *should* have handled that situation better!" Would you tell them, "If you really wanted to succeed bad enough, you would already be a success"?

Although some would call that tough love, it's not. It's unenlightened and misguided thinking. I'm all for being straightforward—but I'm not for tapping into guilt, shame and fear. Why not learn to tap into your natural ability to learn and grow by removing the obstacles of judgment and criticism?

If you want to motivate yourself in a healthy way that produces long-term results, master your self-talk and communicate with yourself in a way that brings out the best in you. Remember…

Your self-talk leads to your emotions, your emotions lead to your decisions, your decisions lead to your behaviors and your behaviors lead to your results.

The last word in the last sentence is "results." To

change the results in your life, change your self-talk. Here are two things to think about:

- When you think or feel you cannot do something, ask your Higher Self if that's your past programming talking.

- When you want to change your emotional state, change your self-talk.

You've probably heard the phrase *Inner Critic* before. Many coaches, therapists and authors advise you to "conquer" or "silence" your inner critic. Some even recommend telling your inner critic to shut up. They believe your inner critic is bad somehow and you have to resist it and control it. That's bad advice and here's why:

If you get into a fight with yourself, you're going to lose the fight. Please understand your inner critic is not your enemy and its intent isn't to criticize you. Your inner critic has a positive intent—it's actually trying to help you. Instead of fighting and resisting your inner critic, get to know it and make friends with it.

Have a conversation with that aspect of yourself and develop a *partnership* with it. How can you do that? Begin by thanking your inner critic for doing its best to help you have a better life and let it know how much you appreciate its positive intent. Here's an example of a conversation with an "inner critic."

Bob: Hello. I'm wondering if you're willing to talk for a minute? I know I've been ignoring you and I apologize for that. I'd really like for us to talk and get to know each other."

Inner Critic ("IC" from here on): Why should I talk to you? Like you said, you've been ignoring me. You've also yelled at me and told me to shut up."

Bob: I know. I'm sorry about that. I'm learning some

new things and I need your help. One of the new things I've learned is you've been trying to help me all these years. I want to thank you for that.

IC: Okay, I didn't see that one coming, but I have to tell you, it's nice to be appreciated.

Bob: I'm really happy we're talking. Would you tell me the positive intent behind what I've thought was you just criticizing me?

Now back to you. Have a conversation with yourself. Imagine you have all these different aspects of yourself and one of them is your inner critic. Talk with it and you'll be surprised what you discover and how you can find ways to connect and collaborate.

A good question to ask your inner critic or another aspect of yourself you've typically fought with (such as your "Fearful Self" or "Inner Perfectionistic") is, "Would you be willing to work together to find a way to get the outcome you want? I'd like to work together to find a way that's more effective."

I know all this takes some imagination, and you have plenty of that. When you worry or when you criticize yourself, you're using your imagination in a less than useful way. Using your imagination in the way I'm suggesting makes you feel good, competent and powerful.

Remind yourself that everything you do is done from a positive intent. If that statement doesn't ring true for you right now, that's okay. We've been taught that we sabotage ourselves. We've also been told over and over again we're our own worst enemy.

What does that thinking lead to? That's right—to more self-criticism. Yes, we can sabotage ourselves—and we do at times. But that's not what we're trying to do—that's not our *intent*. I believe everything you do has a positive intent—you're doing the best you can in the moment to get your needs met in some way.

How you choose to do that doesn't always have

positive consequences, but the intent is positive. Your inner critic is trying to help you, not to sabotage you. As you build a relationship with your inner critic—and all other aspects of self—you will find that life gets easier and easier.

How to Change Your Self-talk:

Below is a template from cognitive behavioral psychology—an effective model for changing your beliefs and self-talk. If you use this tool for even five minutes a day, you will see results.

The A-B-C-D-E Model.

"A" = "Activating Event" - It could be a thought you have or an external event. Whenever you feel an emotion, "positive" or "negative," something has "activated" it.

"B" = "Beliefs" - Your beliefs about "A" and your ongoing self-talk about "A."

"C" = "Emotional Consequences" - How you feel as a result of the self-talk you write down in "B."

"D" = "Dispute" - Question, challenge and "dispute" what you write down for "B."

"E" = "Exchange" - Exchange your old beliefs and self-talk with more useful self-talk and beliefs.

Here are the cliff notes on mastering your emotions: By far, most people think external events and situations determine their emotional response. In other words, "A" causes "B." However, external events ("A") don't create our internal emotions ("C")—our self-talk ("B") does.

In other words: *What you say to yourself makes you feel the way you do at any given moment.* If you want to change how you feel about yourself or about situations in your life, change your self-talk.

Below is an example of how to use the "A-B-C-D-E Model" to change your beliefs, perspectives and self-talk.

Coaching Suggestion: When you use this model, start with "A," skip "B" and go directly to "C," then come back to "B."

"A" - Write out the Activating Event

- "I weighed myself on the scales."

"B" - Beliefs or self-talk about "A"

- "I just can't lose weight."
- "I have failed every time I've tried to stick to an exercise program."
- "It's too hard to lose weight and get fit."
- "I'm so undisciplined—what's wrong with me?"
- "I might as well just give up."

"C" - Write down how you feel—your emotional consequences from what you wrote in "B"

- Discouraged
- Angry
- Depressed and even hopeless about losing weight
- Ashamed
- Stuck

"D" - Dispute your self-talk and beliefs.

Come up with different ways of looking at your situation. Question, challenge and dispute what you wrote for "B." Is what you wrote for "B" the "truth"? Can you prove it to be true or is it just your belief? How accurate or inaccurate is your thinking? Better yet, how useful or less than useful is your belief, perspective or thinking? Is your self-talk empowering or disempowering?

- "I seem to be saying that the past equals the future, but part of me knows that's not true, even if it feels that way."

- "There are plenty of people who have tried many times to lose weight and didn't reach their goal until they tried one more time and finally succeeded. That can be me."

- "In the past, I've always tried to do this alone without any support. Maybe if I got some support it would make a big difference."

- "I just haven't figured out what will work for me and my body when it comes to losing weight. I will try something different and see what happens."

"E" - Exchange your old beliefs and self-talk for something more useful. You can use something you wrote in the "D" section or come up with something else.

- "If others can get healthier and trim down, that would suggest I can too."

- "The past doesn't equal the future. I will get a new plan, get support and keep my mind on what I want instead of thinking about past failures."

Now that you know the power of your self-talk and

have the tools to master your thinking, beliefs and self-talk, you are ready to start mastering your self-talk. **Be patient and loving with yourself because you are learning a new skill.** It takes effort and time to rewire your brain and reprogram your subconscious mind.

Take the time and do the work to develop your ability to step back and change your self-talk when you are in a tough place. When you shift your self-talk (and therefore your perspective) you will find that your circumstances begin to shift as well. The people, resources and solutions you need to transform your life will begin to show up.

Coaching Resource: Thinking Traps

As you pay attention to your self-talk, remember that there are many "thinking traps" we can fall into. In cognitive behavioral psychology these thinking patterns are called ANTS—Automatic Negative Thoughts.

- *Premature Closure*: This happens when you reach a conclusion and close your mind to anything that conflicts with your conclusion. Concluding "I can't do this" is a classic example of premature closure. The *Merck Manual* for healthcare professionals states premature closure is one of the most common mistakes doctors and nurses make: They make a fast diagnosis and stop gathering needed information.

- *Mind-Reading:* "Mind-reading is when you believe you know what someone thinks or feels—even though they haven't told you what they're thinking or feeling.

- *Labeling:* This is when you accept a label for on yourself or others: "What do you expect, he's a Millennial." Labeling leads to premature closure: "I'm lazy," "I'm shy," "I'm fearful," "I'm not good enough," I'm unmotivated," "I'm a failure," "I'm selfish," "I'm not-so-smart," or "I'm a klutz." These are labels you took on without thinking it through and considering the evidence that tells you the label isn't appropriate for you.

These labels then become a part of your self-identity. There is a big difference between saying "I'm undisciplined" and saying "I often don't follow through." The truth is you follow through on more things than you give yourself credit for. Even if that weren't true, don't confuse your behavior with who you are.

- *"Should" Thinking:* This is when you use words like "should," "ought," "should have" and "have to." As in, "I *have* to lose weight." "I *should* be doing better in my career." The late Dr. Albert Ellis called this "shoulding" all over yourself. It's not a pretty metaphor but it gets the point across. When you use words such as "should," "must," "have to" or any phrase that takes choice away from you, you create unnecessary internal resistance.

- *Discounting the Positive:* You do this when you minimize your achievements, your progress or the positive things others think and say about you. "I guess I did okay in my presentation at work, but I *could have* done better." "Oh, this outfit? I've had it for a while now, but thank you."

- *Emotional Reasoning:* You engage in emotional reasoning when you assume your feelings and emotions reflect reality. "If I feel like I'm not good enough, that must mean I'm not." "If I was smart and capable, I would feel confident. Since I often don't feel confident, I must not be smart and capable."

- *All or Nothing Thinking:* Often called black or white

thinking, it means we fail to see that everything is on a continuum. For instance, if someone dislikes something about you, there is no room in your thinking to realize they also like many things about you. Another example of all or nothing thinking is "I'm either a success or a failure."

- *Fortune Teller Thinking:* This is the cause of almost all anxiety and worry. In this thinking trap you predict a negative outcome such as "I'm not going to do well in my new role at work." Or, you predict your boss will reject your request for a raise so you go into the discussion expecting to be turned down.

- *"Awfulizing":* That's the fancy psychological term for heavy duty worrying. Another term we use for this thinking trap is *Catastrophic Thinking* and it's often paired with *Fortune Teller Thinking*. That happens when you predict something in the future will be terrible in some way. You "awfulize" something when you "make a mountain out of a molehill."

  Awfulizing and *Fortune Teller Thinking* are responsible for procrastination. We put things off because we predict the task will be more difficult or unpleasant than it would actually be. We "awfulize" situations when we make them worse in our thinking than they really are. If something is challenging, your job is to make certain you maintain perspective, avoiding making things worse than they are.

- *"I Can't Stand-It-Itis":* You engage in this thinking trap when you tell yourself, "I can't stand this" or "I hate this" ("I hate exercising") or when you say to yourself, "I can't stand being rejected." Telling yourself, "I can't handle this" is another way of saying you can't stand it. The fact is you *can* stand it and the proof is you've stood it in the past. You don't like it because it's unpleasant, but you can stand it. Just because you feel you can't handle something doesn't mean you can't and won't.

- *Mental Filter:* The "This Is Bad" filter and "This Is Good" filter we discussed earlier are examples of this thinking trap. When you put an event or something about yourself through the mental filter of "Bad" or "Not Good Enough" you will feel miserable, anxious, frustrated or stuck. *Abundance Thinking* would be a filter that empowers you and *Poverty* or *Scarcity Thinking* would be filters that disempower you and make life a matter of surviving rather than thriving.

- *Overgeneralization:* Instead of seeing events or your personal qualities as one thing among many, you generalize them. For instance, if you're not good at math, that means you're not as smart as others. If you fail a few times, you turn that into "I usually fail in life." The truth is you succeed with many things every day but fail to acknowledge it.

The bottom line is it pays to pay attention to your self-talk. Self-talk, beliefs and thinking patterns can be so subtle you don't even notice them. That's why they're called ANTS—Automatic Negative Thoughts—because they're automatic. You're used to them and you're not aware of them.

Our thoughts and self-talk might be what water is to fish or the air we breathe is to us—we are so used to it we don't even notice it. There's a story about an older and wiser fish that came upon several younger fish and asked, "So how's the water today?" The younger and not so aware fish replied, "Water? What's that?" They were born in the water and had lived their entire life in it. It was so much a part of them they just weren't aware of it.

Remember, the third secret to *Enlightened Happiness* is **Master Your Self-Talk, Master Your Life.**

For now, think about this:

"Just because you believe something doesn't make it a fact."
- Alan Allard

"The voice that you hear most often and the voice that has the most power and impact on you is your own self-talk."
- Alan Allard

"You are the world's greatest hypnotist when it comes to hypnotizing yourself."
- Alan Allard

"Don't believe your beliefs."
- Unknown

"Both poverty and riches are the offspring of thought."
- Napoleon Hill

SECRET FOUR: SELF-CONFIDENCE FULES YOUR SUCCESS

"Life shrinks or expands in proportion to ones courage."
- Anais Nin

"Learning too soon our limitations, we never learn our powers."
- Mignon McLaughlin

The fourth secret to *Enlightened Happiness* is **Self-Confidence Fuels Your Success.** Nothing can replace self-confidence, especially when you need it the most. To be happy you have to believe in yourself enough to know you can become and achieve what you want.

Self-talk and self-confidence go hand in hand. As you master talking to yourself in an empowering and nurturing way, your self-confidence will grow deeper and stronger than you can imagine.

Confidence is important because if you want to be happier you have to be able to challenge yourself to keep learning, growing and to step out of your comfort zone. Otherwise you become complacent—and complacency robs you of happiness. Self-confidence allows you to think big, to dream and to take action to build an extraordinary life.

You can feel powerful and worthy because *you can learn to feel that way*. But what do you do while you are learning to believe in yourself and learning to feel your power? What do you do when you're not feeling capable and powerful? Many coaches tell us to "fake it until you make it." However, that's not necessary and here's why:

If you attempt something—even if you feel like you're faking it—*you're not faking it*. You're using what confidence you have to get out of your comfort zone and take a risk. *There's nothing fake about that, so give yourself the credit you are due.* Move forward with the confidence you have while feeding that confidence and building it.

If you don't have the confidence you want, you're not alone. And if you're a woman, there's evidence that confidence is a bigger problem for women than men, although it's a significant problem for men too. Whether you're a woman or a man, building your self-confidence and sense of self-worth every day is one of the smartest things you can do for yourself.

Confidence allows us to acknowledge our fears, mistakes and weaknesses, and to embrace them with patience, empathy and understanding. An enlightened level of confidence doesn't allow guilt or shame to erode our confidence and sense of self-worth. It doesn't force us to pretend that we have it all together. You know as well as I do that no one has it *all* together.

Enlightened self-confidence allows us to be human and to own that we are on a journey filled with missteps, stumbles and even full-on crashes at times. However, enlightened confidence tells us that we will *never* eliminate all our weaknesses and turn them into strengths. Enlightened confidence knows it doesn't matter—it knows *we move forward by focusing on our assets, not our deficits.*

You might be wondering, "If I have this confidence

inside, why don't I feel it more often?" It's because in the past you've paid more attention to your doubts, fears and self-criticism than you paid attention to your strengths, successes and to the progress you made. When you did that, your self-confidence took a hit.

What usually registers first and makes the biggest impression on you—a success or a "failure"? Would it be easier for you to make a list of your weaknesses, mistakes and deficits than it would be to make a list of your positive characteristics, achievements and successes? Most people would say that the first list is bigger and comes to mind quicker than the second list. It's no wonder that deeper self-confidence eludes so many of us.

Another reason you lack more confidence and don't feel powerful is because you get hypnotized by your circumstances. It's as if your outer circumstances are saying, "You're no match for me—don't even try to change me." However, there is an aspect of you that knows you are strong, capable and amazing in every way. The more you listen to that message, the more confident you will be.

Your confidence empowers you to see past your problems, setbacks and difficulties. It moves you into action when logic and reason tell you to be "realistic" and give up.

Refuse to be hypnotized into believing things will never change. Instead, think like the late movie mogul Samuel Goldwyn, who said, *"It's absolutely impossible—but it has possibilities."* There are some people who actually think and live that way—and you can be one of them.

Self-confidence isn't a luxury in life—it's essential to you living the life you were meant to live. You deserve to know deep down you are capable of not only *imagining* great things—you are capable of *doing* great things. Very few things eat away at us like timidity or fear do. Both fester and spread through mind, spirit and body until we get used to it and no longer notice the small lives we lead.

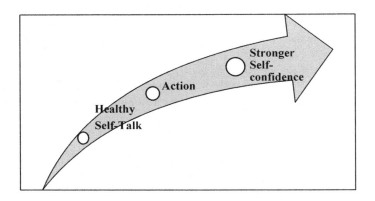

Nurture your self-confidence because **you have to feel at least confident enough to step up or to speak up to make your presence known.** Start with what confidence you have to take action sooner rather than later. That's how your self-confidence will grow and grow and grow.

As you nurture your self-confidence, trust that it's growing and expanding even if it doesn't seem to be. When you plant seeds into the ground you know you have to give them some time to grow without being able to see the physical evidence of their growth. You simply keep giving them water and sunlight and you know they will come out in due time.

The reason I encourage my clients to read this book and other books they find useful over and over is because your subconscious mind often needs to hear or see something many times before it begins to take it in. When you read this book over and over again it's like planting the "belief seeds" in your subconscious mind and giving them the water and sunlight they need.

When you "plant" new beliefs in your subconscious mind, what you are growing will make the weeds irrelevant. Meanwhile, trust that the plant inside the ground will make its appearance above ground in due time. Everything has a gestation time, including the growth of your self-confidence. Know that your patience will be rewarded.

Have you ever stopped to realize you weren't born knowing how to criticize or second guess yourself? That's something you had to learn to do. You had confidence in yourself and in what you could do and you didn't question it—until you *learned* to do so.

As a young child, you knew what you wanted, you believed in yourself and you set goals and achieved them. It's amazing what we can learn and master when we're not criticizing ourselves.

Think about the things you learned to do early in life that gave you the ability to stand on your own two feet. You knew what you wanted, you believed in yourself and before you knew it, you were off and running. That's how a child learns to walk. They take a few steps, fall down, get up and fall again and again. Sometimes they cry a bit after they fall, but they get up again to explore their world.

All the time, children are getting support, praise and encouragement to keep them going. We understand how important that is for them—and we grossly underestimate its importance for adults. How did we ever get to that point of ignorance?

Early in life you understood your worth and it was reinforced by those around you—at least for a while. The problem is that at some point, the encouragement lessened and the limiting messages grew. The former became fainter and the latter grew louder. Eventually you internalized those limiting messages.

Growing up, we heard messages (mostly unintentional) that we were not good enough in some way. We were taught to feel bad about our mistakes and failures and we began to equate our mistakes with self. That's what happened to my client Bob. He had an extremely abusive father who would tell him that he was a mistake in life and that he would never succeed at anything. Bob's father often told Bob that he was stupid and worthless. He also told him that he was an "ungrateful bastard" and he didn't deserve the good things he had. Thankfully, most of us don't have parents like that.

However, many children (whom are loved dearly) receive conflicting messages through words, tone of voice and facial expressions when mom or dad are angry, such as, "Why can't you just do what you're told?" Perhaps you didn't hear such negative things—but **were you consistently affirmed along the way?**

Many children are taught that there is a right way and a wrong way to do anything and everything—and, of course, many times the child is told their way is the wrong way. They begin to feel there is something wrong with them when they say or do the "wrong" thing.

More than that, they are taught something is wrong with them if they fail to say or do the "right" thing. They learn that when they make a mistake, someone is going to be unhappy with them—and from that *they learn to be unhappy with themselves.*

Their self-esteem, self-worth and self-confidence go down. Over time, their good feelings get smaller and smaller—and their insecurities, doubts and fears get bigger and bigger. Our self-confidence can be undermined in subtle ways. Many years are spent teaching children to conform in order to fit in and they are taught to not ask so many questions.

They learn there's a cost to rocking the boat and they learn authority figures and those in power don't like to be challenged. As a result, their self-confidence gets buried and they begin to expect less and less and to ask for less and less. Their natural curiosity, imagination and fearlessness gives way to settling for "the way things are." Along the way their natural *roar* is muffled.

Initially, children know what they want and they keep asking for what they want until they get it. Then "life" happens to them and they began to tell themselves they don't really want much. What about you? What is your self-confidence like?

Is it singing and dancing—or hiding underneath hurts and disappointments? Have past experiences and your self-talk dampened your inner fire? Have you scaled down what you want in life, all in the name of being "reasonable"?

The challenge is we're bombarded with conflicting messages:

- "Don't get a big head!"
- "You need to be humble."
- "So, you think you're better than everyone else?"
- "Pride comes before the fall."
- "Who do you think you are?"
- "You're being selfish."

These warnings are endless and they create fear, uncertainty and hesitation—when what you need is self-confidence. Your level of self-confidence and self-trust determines whether you take risks and play big or stay in your comfort zone and play small. Self-confidence explains why some people get ahead, some march in place and some fall behind.

> **"The Universe doesn't care if you ask for a little or a lot. Abundance is for everyone, but you have to believe in your own worth."**

Think about what changes you would like to make in your life—then think about how much confidence you have or don't have to make those changes. Know that your confidence is within and you can pay attention to it, nurture it and be grateful for the confidence you do have—and see your confidence soar.

The more you notice times you are confident and

honor that confidence, the stronger and more powerful it gets. It's true that what we focus on tends to expand. What do you focus on in your life? What do you notice the most in your life?

Practice focusing on:
- Your strengths
- What you are grateful for
- You achievements
- Your values
- Your growth and progress
- What you like about yourself

Coaching Assignment: Write down five things that identify either a strength you have, a positive personal characteristic or something you've achieved in life:

1. _____
2. _____
3. _____
4. _____
5. _____

Focusing on what you've written above and on similar things will grow your self-confidence and develop your "I can do this" mindset.

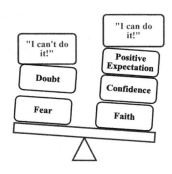

The key is to keep nurturing your self-confidence just like you would water your plants every day. The great thing is you don't have to eliminate all your doubts, fears or "limiting beliefs;" that's impossible. All you have to do is to have a *little* more confidence than your doubts and fears. You do that by nurturing your confidence, not by trying to eliminate your doubts and fears.

Here are four ways to get the fire of your self-confidence roaring (and if you find yourself thinking, "I already know this," ask yourself, "Am I *doing* it?"):

1) Be Your Own Measuring Stick

Far too many people live their life feeling they are not smart enough, good enough, capable enough or attractive enough. I'm talking about people others consider very capable, smart and attractive. Often, they feel that way after they've compared themselves to someone else—and decided they're not as good as that person is in some area.

Dan called me for his coaching session frustrated and discouraged—straight from a "weight loss" group. When I asked him how he did, he said he had lost a quarter of a pound. Then he said, "What's a quarter of a pound when five others in my group lost one to two pounds?" Dan was unhappy all because he compared himself to others in a way that worked against him.

It's fine to compare yourself to others, *if you do it in a way that inspires you.* Otherwise, **your progress should be measured against yourself; not against others.** You need to be your own measuring stick. When you do that, you will see yourself and your life in a different light and your confidence will begin to rise.

2) Celebrate Yourself

Do you ever hear an inner voice saying something like

"I *should* do better," "I *need* to do better" or "*If only* I had more discipline"? Can you feel the self-criticism, perfectionism and unenlightened thinking here?

If you feel you aren't capable of achieving what you really want—a *calling* instead of a job, starting your own business, writing a book or reaching a healthy weight goal—**that's your perfectionism speaking**. It's telling you you're not good enough to be or to achieve what you want. It's time to begin talking to yourself in a supportive and affirming way.

Learn to celebrate who you are and make it a habit to celebrate your efforts—even when you "fail." What can you celebrate when you fail? How about your courage to do what you did? How about celebrating what you learned along the way? Perfectionistic thinking robs you of your opportunity to celebrate your small successes by discounting them or by comparing them to the success of others.

Most people could stand to ease up on themselves. The challenge is that when you're down on yourself (perfectionism) it's tempting to think you need to be even harder on yourself. You think, "The problem is I've been too easy on myself. I need to raise my standards and do whatever it takes to meet them—no excuses."

Your self-criticism wears you down and makes it ten times harder to do the very thing you demand of yourself. Then you ask, *"What's wrong with me?"* or you think, "*I need to be more disciplined and just do it!"* When you get caught up in these kinds of thoughts, take a breath and say to yourself: **"My self-criticism kills my self-confidence"**

Criticism comes at a terrible price and has a short shelf-life when it comes to improving your performance—if it does at all. The more enlightened approach of self-acceptance and self-love creates the positive energy you need to perform at your best.

Simply put, self-love will fuel your happiness—and success. You might feel that self-love and self-acceptance is soft stuff, but the truth is, for most people, it's not soft stuff—it's the hard stuff.

Focus on your strengths and remind yourself of your past achievements, big and small. Take a look at yourself through the eyes of those who like, love and respect you. Celebrate yourself, feel good about yourself and each time *you will get a happiness boost.*

The truth is, the happier you are with yourself the more successful you will be. Being happy will make it easier for you to be successful, while being "successful" doesn't always lead to happiness.

3) Build Your Own Fan Club

Does the idea of having your own fan club make you uncomfortable? If so, why? Does it seem to be a little narcissistic? Why is that? We need people around us to believe in us and support our goals and aspirations.. Everyone you interact with either makes a deposit or a withdrawal in your self-confidence bank account.

I have had many clients who were in a primary relationship that drug them down. One client that comes to mind was a sales professional that used to be in the top ten percent of her industry. When she began coaching, her work was suffering. When I asked her to consider how her boyfriend was dragging her down, she said, "I don't want to blame anyone or any circumstance on my performance at work." It took her a while to see how misguided that was—but she eventually did and she ended the relationship.

I'm all for taking responsibility, but not for being *over-responsible*. My client was blaming herself for being human. Yes, I know we're responsible for our own emotional health. But unless you're a machine, the people you're close to will either build you up or tear you down.

If you're in a difficult relationship and you don't get it turned around, it will suck the life right out of you over time. It might take a year or it might take ten years, but sooner or later you will pay the price for staying in a relationship that wears you down. **Telling yourself to rise above these kinds of things is perfectionism and self-abuse.**

If you're around someone you have to work hard to get along with and enjoy being with, something is wrong. It's up to you to take the initiative to correct that. If you can't, it's time to let go of the relationship and wish the person well. It's time to protect yourself and only be around those who help you be your best self and bring the best out of you.

You need to be around those who "get" who you are. You need to be around those who are excited about the vision you have for your life. You want confidence boosters, not confidence busters.

For a while now, I've been a part of what is called a "Master-Mind" group. We meet weekly or every other week (in person or by phone/skype) and share our successes, mistakes and failures and we support each other with ideas, challenge each other and bring out the best in each other. I wouldn't be where I am today without these relationships.

You don't have to build a big fan club but if you want to be happier, you need the right people in your life—even if it's a small number. Get them, love them and be their raving fan in return. That way, everyone wins.

4) Challenge Yourself

Your self-confidence won't grow if you don't challenge yourself to go beyond where you are now. Think of going to the gym—if you don't challenge your muscles, they won't grow. It's the same with your self-confidence. If you want more of the things life has for you, you have to understand they are waiting for you outside your comfort zone.

Why do you have to move out of your comfort zone? Because if you don't yet have something you want, it's possible what you want is waiting for you—outside your comfort zone.

Don't get me wrong. There's nothing wrong with enjoying being in your comfort zone. The problem comes when you stay in it too long. *No one stays outside their comfort zone all of the time or even most of the time. The key is to step outside it often enough to experiment, take calculated risks and to stretch yourself.* If that appeals to you, here's how to go about it:

Choose an area of your life and set a specific goal that stretches you at least a bit. Go to the edge of what you think you can be and do and then step over that line. If you want to be more assertive, look for ways to practice being assertive in easier situations first. Tell a trusted friend you are working on being assertive and ask him or her to help you to be more assertive with them.

The key is to take small and easy steps at first. What's a small step that's so easy to take you're almost guaranteed success? That's the way to start getting out of your comfort zone and creating the experiences and results that will change your life for the better.

Remember, the fourth secret to Enlightened Happiness is **Self-confidence Fuels Your Success.** Here are the four ways to increase your self-confidence:

- **Only Compare Yourself to Yourself**
- **Celebrate Yourself**
- **Build Your Own Fan Club**
- **Challenge Yourself**

Think about the following to grow your self-confidence:

"Nothing splendid has ever been achieved except by those who dared believe that something inside of them was superior to circumstance."
- Bruce Barton

"Those who mind, don't matter, and those who matter don't mind."
- Bernard M. Baruch

"I had a boyfriend who told me I'd never succeed, never be nominated for a Grammy, never have a hit song, and that he hoped I'd fail. I said to him, 'Someday when we're not together, you won't be able to order a cup of coffee at the deli without hearing or seeing me.'"
- Lady Gaga

"What a man thinks of himself, that it is which determines his fate."
- Henry David Thoreau

"Self-Confidence is the first requisite to great undertaking."
- Samuel Johnson

As soon as you trust yourself, you will know how to live."
- Johann Wolfgang von Goethe

"Fear defeats more people than any other one thing in the world."
- Ralph Waldo Emerson

"Control your own destiny or someone else will."
- Jack Welch

SECRET FIVE: THERE IS NO SUBSTITUTE FOR SELF-LOVE

"Of all the judgments we pass in life, none is more important than the judgment we pass on ourselves."
- Nathaniel Branden

"The most terrifying thing is to accept oneself completely."
- Carl Jung

The fifth secret to *Enlightened Happiness* is **There Is No Substitute for Self-Love.** Your ability to accept and embrace who you are affects everything in your life. Many people struggle with accepting and loving themselves but *don't realize they struggle with it.* Here are some signs of a lack of self-love:

- Settling for less than you deserve in your relationships
- Falling short of your career potential
- Failing to take care of your health
- Difficulty getting along with others
- Not knowing what you want
- Lack of assertiveness
- Passive-aggressiveness
- Money issues—lack and scarcity thinking

- Being unhappy in general
- Depression
- Self-criticism
- Difficulty accepting compliments
- Being too hard on yourself

The most important relationship you will ever have is your relationship with yourself. Everything you experience in life flows from how you view and feel about yourself. In fact, I would go so far as to say, you need to fall in love with yourself all over again.

If that sounds narcissistic, it's not. As a former psychotherapist, I can tell you that narcissism isn't about loving yourself too much—it's about the opposite—it's about a lack of self-worth and self-love. A narcissistic person can't hear anything negative about himself or herself—it's just too painful for them. Why? Because they don't have a foundation of self-love and self-respect.

That also explains why they don't take responsibility for their mistakes or shortcomings. They don't have the self-esteem to take responsibility so they have to come across as if they're perfect. They're never the problem; it's always someone else. It takes self-esteem and self-worth to own your mistakes, shortcomings and failures.

Narcissism isn't a problem for most people. However, far too many people, for other reasons, worry about what others think of them and they get upset over how others treat them. *Meanwhile, they pay little to no attention to how they think of themselves and how they treat themselves.* That's tragic because you have to love yourself to expect others to treat you well.

If you aren't happy with yourself now, learning how to love yourself, accept yourself and support yourself should be your first priority. It's difficult to give to others and to be there for them when your own life has too much frustration, disappointment and pain.

Some authors and coaches tell us we shouldn't pursue

happiness because happiness is elusive when we make it our goal. A recent blog post I read on happiness said, "The more you search for happiness, the less you will find of it." That's just plain wrong.

It's true that happiness or even self-love eludes us when we pursue them in ways that don't work—money, prestige and power won't make you happy or increase your self-love. There are plenty of people who have an abundance of all that and feel little happiness or self-love. So happiness and self-love are slippery when we try to get them in ways that don't work—but that doesn't mean you shouldn't make your happiness and your ability to love yourself your highest priorities.

Learning to accept yourself and give yourself what you need to thrive in life will make you happy. That's why self-love is the place to start if you want more happiness. With that in mind, I suggested earlier it's time to fall in love with yourself all over again. Does that make you uncomfortable?

You have a right to feel like you are an absolutely incredible person. You have a right to feel worthy of love, health, abundance and prosperity. To feel all that, you have to love yourself, accept yourself and support yourself unconditionally. You deserve that.

Do you see yourself as a creative force of power in the universe capable of co-creating whatever you desire? If you struggle with feeling not good enough, smart enough or capable enough, you're not alone. I had to deal with this earlier in my life and I can tell you that countless others have as well.

The famous author Maya Angelou commented once about her struggles with accepting her worth and talent, saying, "I have written eleven books, but each time I think, 'Uh oh, they're going to find out now. I've run a game on everybody, and they're going to find me out.'"

If you know anything about Oprah Winfrey, you know she has shared her struggles with self-worth and self-confidence. Many other accomplished, famous and wealthy people have struggled with their self-esteem and with loving themselves. Meryl Streep said that at times she would think, "Why would anyone want to see me again in a movie? And I don't know how to act anyway, so why am I doing this?"

Actor Mike Myers said, "At any time, I still think the no-talent police will come and arrest me." There is a name for what we are talking about; it's called the *Imposter Syndrome* or *Imposter Phenomenon*. Researchers at Georgia State University coined this term in the late 1970's. I've had a number of clients who had a lot of wealth, big titles and power who felt like they were "imposters" who would be found out.

Not feeling good enough, capable enough or smart enough isn't just an indication of a lack of confidence; it's a sign of a lack of self-love and self-worth. **No one has reached the pinnacle of self-love**. There is always room to grow when it comes to your beliefs about yourself and your worth.

However, many people who struggle with self-love aren't aware of their struggle. We want to say, "Of course I love myself," when asked about it. It's not that we don't love ourselves to varying degrees or we don't feel worthy at all—it's that there is still work to be done.

We all have some amount of baggage we still carry around in life—baggage that gets in the way of our ability to unleash our hidden potential. Developing your self-awareness and your capacity to love and unconditionally accept yourself is key to releasing your potential. Any work you do in this area will have a dramatic return on investment.

Karen, a former client of mine, once told me, "I think the whole idea of loving yourself is overblown. I'm so tired of hearing about self-love. I know some people who love themselves so much they can't hear anything but praise." Many would agree with what Karen said. She's right that the topics of self-love and self-esteem have gotten a lot of attention over the years. However, the question isn't whether we've heard the message; the question is, "Have we taken the message to heart?

Why does the topic of self-love seem to be so difficult for so many of us? One reason is we receive conflicting messages about self-love from many psychotherapists, psychologists, pastors, priests and others. Many of them say that we need to focus on others, not on self. I've heard it expressed this way: "Be other-centered, not self-centered."

The problem with that advice is that until you get your own needs met you won't have the reserve you need to give to others. **You have to fill your own tank first.**

Do we need to think of others and to meet their needs? Certainly. But relationships are based on reciprocity, on giving and receiving—they can't be a one way street. If you give too much of yourself and you don't receive what others can give you, you won't have anything left to give. This truth shows up in many ways.

A controlling husband or wife isn't controlling because they have enough self-love; it's quite the opposite. They have emotional, psychological and spiritual (having to do with the human spirit) needs they might not even be aware of, or if they are, they don't know how to get them met.

They might have a need to be right all the time or to feel more powerful than the other person. So they try to get their needs met the best way they know how—by being controlling.

Why do we learn ineffective ways to meet our needs? To answer that question we have to go back to our earlier, formative years when we developed our core beliefs and values—the ones that explain our behaviors today. Often, what limits us today are the beliefs we learned long ago that serve as internal "brakes" on our journey of discovery, change and growth.

Our internal brakes aren't fully engaged, but they're on

enough to slow us down and create unnecessary stress. If you want to move forward, you have to take your foot off of your mental, emotional and spiritual brakes. What brakes are those, you ask?

- Self-criticism
- Ongoing self-doubt
- Criticizing others
- Relationships that hold us back
- Taking care of others but not self
- Staying in your comfort zone
- Isolating yourself
- Procrastination
- Burying or numbing your emotions
- Thinking based on fear, scarcity and lack
- Settling for less than we are capable of achieving or being

All of us enter adulthood with our mental, emotional and spiritual brakes on to some degree. Otherwise, we would be more free, more daring—and happier. We would be crystal clear on what we *really* want, we would believe we could create the life we want and we would take consistent action.

But reality says that most of us are not quite there yet. In actuality, there are a number of things that keep us from thriving in our lives and careers—such as fear, guilt and shame. These are all common struggles that often go undetected.

Perhaps you struggle to some degree with feeling or thinking, "I should do better!" "What's wrong with me?" or "I could have done better." These are shame-based thoughts and feelings—and they usually go undetected. **Love and acceptance encourages and supports, it doesn't accuse and shame.**

My experience tells me that when people think things

like "I *should* do better," or "I *need* to change this," their next step is often to push themselves harder. Their self-talk includes statements such as, "I'd better get my act together" and "I only have myself to blame."

Of course, their intent is good; they're trying to motivate themselves to be better and to do better. However, being harder on themselves doesn't work, even if it seems to at times. If you think it does, take a look at how it has worked for you in the long term.

If you think about it, you might have felt a temporary burst of "motivation" that soon faded away, leaving you feeling worse. Perhaps you improved some behavior for a while, but for how long? We know intuitively that we need love and acceptance but we often subconsciously choose to be self-critical or to push ourselves harder instead.

Even though it doesn't work, we either think it does or we do it because it's what we know and what we're comfortable with. However, it might be good for us to ask ourselves if continuing to do what's comfortable in the short term will give us comfort in the long term.

It won't and here's why: If someone criticizes you or "pushes" you psychologically or emotionally—how are you going to respond? Unless you really trust them and you're secure in yourself, you will push back. If you're too timid to push back in a direct way, you will do it indirectly with passive-aggressive behavior.

It works the same way when you try to make yourself do something you don't really want to do. You don't like being forced into anything, so you resist and push back. The bottom line is if you push yourself—when what you need is encouragement—you will find a way to fight back.

That's why "willpower" only goes so far; you're trying to make yourself do something you don't want to do. Unless you find your own reasons to truly want to do something, trying to make yourself do it backfires on you. Think about this in relation to the workplace. Leaders who are enlightened choose to inspire others instead of pushing them.

More and more leaders (those I call "enlightened leaders") are learning how to coach their team because they know that coaching starts from discovering what an employee is already motivated to do. If what the employee wants is aligned with what the organization wants, magic happens.

Trying to make employees do what they don't want to do does work on some level—and that's why we still do that so often in the workplace. However, that will never lead to exceptional performance. Enlightened leaders have *learned* how to inspire their team rather than drive them.

Now, back to you and the madness of trying to make yourself do what you don't really want to do. What can we do instead of trying to *make* ourselves do better or be better? Part of loving and accepting yourself is to identify your strengths and passions and to find a way to unleash them in life and at work.

Anything less is some level of trying to make yourself want to do what you're not built for. You can't put a square peg in a round hole, although many of us do our best to do just that. Especially when it comes to the workplace. That's what we've learned to do and we'll keep doing it until we learn something that works better.

The problem is that many people don't consciously know what they would love to do at work or even in life. To make it more complicated, we've become so busy and distracted we find it hard to find the time to discover what would make us happier at work and in life. If you can relate to that, what can you do about it?

Loving yourself includes making self-awareness a priority and giving yourself what you need to discover what you want. If that means you need to prioritize the time to read relevant books for your career and life success, self-love tells you that you are worth investing the time and energy to do that. If it means working with an exceptional coach, you have to determine if you're worth the investment.

The challenge is that the process of growing in your ability to love and accept yourself can be messy, frustrating and sometimes painful. What do you do then? What do you do with the uncomfortable emotions? Often we try to distract ourselves from feeling any emotional discomfort or pain.

We overeat, go shopping, isolate ourselves or use alcohol or drugs to feel better. Many of us turn to something more socially acceptable like being a workaholic. In fact, work is one of the most common reasons we give as to why we don't have time to take care of ourselves, time to think about our goals or time to relax and enjoy ourselves.

Many people resist talking about their pain with someone who knows how to help them navigate through their maze of emotions. Too many of us like to keep things bottled up. Yes, I know, many people like to complain non-stop about their pain—but that's another story. Getting help when we're hurting isn't complaining; it's getting help.

Unfortunately, many of us feel it *is* complaining. That stops us from sharing what's going on with us; no one likes to be viewed as a complainer. We would rather be viewed as the strong and silent type or be considered a "positive" person and not a "negative" person.

So we keep it to ourselves. To make matters worse, some tell us that thinking about or speaking of anything "negative" brings more of the same into our lives. It's true we can bring more misery into our life by focusing too much on that pain.

However, the solution isn't to smile and say everything is fine when we're hurting inside. The solution isn't to be miserable and to stay silent. The solution is to find someone who can help you get to where you want to and deserve to be.

Sometimes we're afraid to experience our emotions and

to talk directly about them because we're afraid they will take over and consume us. However, when we repress or suppress what we're feeling or thinking, our emotions will find a way to get our attention. There is a saying that is true: "What you resist, persists." The fact is, unresolved emotions won't just "go away."

Often, we are simply ashamed of what we think and feel and we want to hide it from others—and even ourselves. It takes courage to face and express our emotions because it makes us feel vulnerable and most people aren't comfortable with feeling vulnerable.

We want to feel strong and we want others to respect and admire us. We believe that being vulnerable with others will cause them to think less of us. However, the opposite is true. People aren't drawn to someone who projects an illusion of perfection. They want to be around someone who is transparent and not afraid to be vulnerable.

I have had many clients who in the beginning of their coaching, only talked about their achievements, strengths and what was going well in their career and life. Soon into the coaching, however, they relax and are able to talk about things that aren't going so well. It takes courage to do that.

When they do open up, they often say, "I feel like I doubt myself more now and have more insecurities than I did before you started coaching me." I tell them that is a good thing, and of course, they think I'm crazy. I explain to them that their fears and doubts had always been there—they were just not able to acknowledge them until now.

Being transparent and vulnerable is one way to experience healing, growth and transformation. When you open up to the right person, you find out that you are not alone in how you think and feel and that fosters self-acceptance. Additionally, you grow in your ability to process your emotions, accept them and learn from them.

What else can you do to foster your ability to love and accept yourself? You can learn to listen to yourself with grace and love. Grace and love empowers you to listen, empathize and validate whatever you might be thinking or feeling. **Listening to yourself with grace and love will give you a quiet confidence that is amazing and it will unleash your powerful self.**

Criticizing yourself for what you call "negative" emotions doesn't help; it makes things worse. Don't criticize, suppress or deny any of your emotions. All of our emotions are positive in the sense they contain information and messages to guide us.

Learn from your emotions so you can be more self-aware. Times of fear, worry, anxiety, shame, guilt, self-doubt and the feeling that you're not good enough are all important messages. When you allow yourself to feel whatever it is you feel, *without judgment*, you will develop clarity and allow your power to emerge.

How do you learn to allow yourself to experience whatever it is you feel, without judgment? Opening up to someone who can listen without judgment is key. They can help you understand you are not your emotions. Your emotions are what you create internally through your beliefs and thinking, but they are not you. Never confuse the two.

There is never a need to feel guilt or shame for what you might be feeling. Accept your emotions and they will no longer have the power over you they have had in the past. To accept your emotions, it's also helpful to remind yourself your emotions come from your beliefs and thoughts—*all of which you learned somewhere along the way*.

Is it reasonable to beat yourself up for certain beliefs and ways of thinking you learned when you were six years old? Of course, many people do that because they were taught to do just that early on in life. More than once, they heard "You should be ashamed for thinking that" or "Where on earth did you learn to think such a horrible thing?"

Again, is it reasonable to judge yourself for something you learned growing up? Wouldn't it be more reasonable and fair to ask yourself if you would like to have a different belief or to experience a different emotion? Then you could imagine what that would be. How much easier would that make your life?

When you blame yourself for what you're feeling, you're likely to push your emotions down, distract yourself from them or deal with them in other less than useful ways. **By acknowledging *and* accepting we feel powerless, depressed or afraid, we bypass the resistance and invite our powerful self to emerge. It might sound crazy, but that's the way it works.**

We can accept and talk about *all* of our emotions, not just the "positive" ones—because there is no such thing as a "negative" emotion. All emotions are "positive"— regardless of whether they feel positive or not. Of course, there are useful and less than useful ways to respond to or talk about our emotions, but that's a different topic.

How do you make talking with someone about what you're thinking and feeling a useful experience? You do that, in part, by being aware of your intent. What are you trying to achieve? Is it to just complain and blame or is it to gain more understanding, compassion and emotional intelligence?

Loving yourself, accepting yourself and valuing yourself doesn't mean you have to always be positive and upbeat. Being human means we experience a full range of human emotions. Again, our emotions contain messages; the question is, do we want to listen and learn?

That being said, where do we begin? What are some practical steps we can take to grow in our self-love and to embrace our worth and value? What can we start with and do a little bit every day that will make a big difference? I'm going to give you ten ways to increase your self-love. They are simple, powerful and effective and I encourage you to pick one and begin to use it.

Coaching Assignment: Use a journal to record what you are doing to grow your ability to love yourself.

Alan's Top Ten Ways to Love and Accept Yourself Now:

1) Shift Your Focus

Most people notice their mistakes, "failures" and what they don't like about themselves and pay little attention to their positives. Make a list of your strengths, values, talent, achievements and progress. Read a few things on your list every day. You want to update your subconscious mind daily about your strengths, positive characteristics and the progress you're making Don't rely on others to give you positive feedback on a consistent basis—give yourself what you need.

2) Forgive yourself—and others

Forgiving yourself or others doesn't mean you condone or minimize hurtful behavior—whether yours or someone else's. It also doesn't mean you allow someone to continue mistreating and hurting you.

Forgiveness is letting go of the need to hurt that person back or to wish harm on them in any way. The reason self-forgiveness is so important is that without it we find ways to subconsciously punish ourselves to make up for what we've done—or for not being "perfect." (Can't think of anything to forgive yourself for? Are you sure?)

3) Use the "WYSTTYBF" Exercise

Remember WYSTTYBF from the chapter on self-talk? As a reminder, it stands for "Would You Say That To

Your Best Friend?" When you judge yourself, ask yourself if you would judge your best friend that way. Why not treat yourself with the same respect you give to those you admire?

Remind yourself that perfection isn't possible—you can respect yourself without it.

4) Celebrate Your Progress and Reward Yourself

When you achieve something or reach a goal, *celebrate it and reward yourself.* Don't wait until you achieve something big, celebrate the small wins along the way and fuel your progress.

When you fail to recognize and celebrate your progress, even your tiny steps forward, you are telling yourself that only heroic effort is worthy of respect. One reason babies and small children learn so quickly is because we encourage every little step they take in their learning and growing process.

5) Document Your Past Achievements

Write them all down (big and small) and allow yourself to enjoy reliving them in your mind—and add to your list every day. When you need a lift, go back and read your list of accomplishments. Remember when you rode your first bike, learned how to tie your shoes or when you asserted yourself when you were afraid to? Remember, in a sense, *all achievements are big achievements.*

6) Develop Your Inner Circle

Surround yourself with those who will bring out the best in you and stay away from those who undermine your self-confidence and self-worth. Never underestimate the power of peer influence. We become like those we spend the most time with; make that work for you.

If that means letting go of some relationships or at least drastically limiting your association with them, do so. You can't afford people in your life who dampen your spirit or dim your light. Nurture the relationships that nurture you and you will continue to evolve into your best self.

7) Grow Your Gratitude

Use the power of thankfulness and gratitude to transform your life. Write down three things a day that you enjoy and appreciate. That could be a person in your life, a past experience, a possession, the cup of coffee you had that day, a compliment you received, and so on.

Nothing is too small to be mindful and appreciative of. It's okay to repeat things from day to day as long as you are being mindful of what you are being thankful for.

8) Master Your Self-Talk

Develop your ability to pay attention to your self-talk throughout the day. Remember that your self-talk will either create positive or negative energy for you.

Learn to talk to yourself in a way that makes you feel alive, powerful and significant. Use your self-talk to fuel your success and to enable you to thrive in life, in all ways.

9) Get Some Fan Letters

Ask three people whom you trust to write you a letter detailing what they like, admire, love and respect about you. Ask them to tell you what they see as your strengths and positives. Ask them to include examples of what they've seen in your life. This will help reveal why they think and feel the way they do about you. By the way, most people won't do what I'm suggesting here. Will you?

10) Take Exquisite Care of Yourself

You are the goose that lays the golden eggs in your life. Give yourself the attention and the care your powerful self will emerge and thrive. You can't give others what you don't have without being depleted. Take care of yourself and give yourself the time and attention you need to thrive and others will begin to treat you the way you deserve.

Remember, the fifth secret to *Enlightened Happiness is* **There Is No Substitute for Self-love.**

Here are a few things to think about:

"The most terrifying thing is to accept oneself completely."
- Carl G. Jung

We fear to know the fearsome and unsavory aspects of ourselves, but we fear even more to know the godlike in ourselves."
- Abraham Maslow

"You can search throughout the entire universe for someone who is more deserving of your love and affection than you are yourself, and that person is not to be found anywhere. You yourself, as much as anybody in the entire universe, deserve your love and affection."
- Buddha

SECRET SIX: GRATITUDE IS THE GREAT HAPPINESS MULTIPLIER

"Acknowledging the good that you already have in your life is the foundation for all abundance."
- Eckhart Tolle

"There are only two ways to live your life. One is as though nothing is a miracle. The other is as though everything is a miracle."
- Albert Einstein

The sixth secret to *Enlightened Happiness* is **Gratitude is the Great Happiness Multiplier.** Here's why: It's impossible to be unhappy when you're feeling grateful and it's impossible to be happy when you're not feeling gratitude. Gratitude isn't a silver bullet for happiness but it is a *shortcut to happiness*.

Gratitude is almost magical in its ability to transform your life because when you notice the wonder and magic in life you just feel better. The more grateful you are for what you have, the more you will have in life to be grateful for. That's because gratitude opens your eyes to possibilities and opportunities and it gives you the motivation to pursue them.

Gratitude is also an effective treatment for depression and anxiety, a problem that's increasing around the globe. Martin Seligman, Ph.D., known for his pioneering work in Positive Psychology, found that gratitude is a powerful prescription for depression, even in the tough cases (Just because something is simple doesn't mean it's easy).

How can gratitude help with something as serious as depression? When we focus on what is "right" in our lives and on what we can feel thankful for—*even on a small level*—our happiness naturally increases. That means you can increase your happiness in small ways that lead to big gains in happiness over time. Focusing on what you are grateful for turns your happiness switch on—and you can do that anytime you choose.

> **"Remember to flip your happiness switch on by focusing on what is good in your life."**

Gratitude isn't the entire answer to the challenges of life, but it's a simple solution that's often overlooked. We often overlook the simple solutions right in front of us. It's easy to take what we have for granted. We have to decide to nurture our gratitude for it to grow and expand.

There are times in everyone's life when it seems that everything has gone wrong and the future looks bleak. If your relationship with your significant other is in trouble, if you're in a lot of debt, if you're having health problems or if your job isn't going well, you have to intentionally and consciously find things to make yourself feel good.

Paying attention to **anything and everything there is to feel good about changes your life.** To do that you have to take charge and tell your brain and your subconscious mind what you want them to notice and focus on. If you put your attention on what's "wrong," what's "missing" what's difficult in your life, your subconscious mind will think you want more of that.

Coaching Assignment: Sit down for a minute or two, close your eyes, and ask yourself this powerful question: "What is in my life I can feel good about right now, even just a little?" The reason I suggest you ask what you feel good about instead of what you feel grateful about is because it's often an easier question to answer than "What do I feel grateful for?" When you ask, "What do I feel good about, even just a little?" and it's also likely to be something you feel some amount of thankfulness for. Then, when the answer(s) pop up, simply say, "Thank you." That's it.

Do that once a day for thirty days and pay attention to what changes. Change will occur, but you have to be awake and pay attention to how things change or you won't notice it.

Seeing what's wrong and focusing on what we don't have is what many people do the most of. In the beginning, my clients don't need any prompting to talk about their frustrations, setbacks and fears. That's understandable because that's what they've learned to do. I remind myself often that "What I focus on and give my energy to, expands."

Ask yourself, "What am I giving my attention and energy to?" Worry and you will get more to worry about. Be negative and you will get more things to be negative about. Criticize and you will get more in your life to criticize. However, the opposite is true as well.

Focus on what you want that you already have, even if it's in your life to a tiny degree. Be thankful for it and watch it grow and multiply. Of course, that doesn't happen by being thankful for five minutes and then spending the next hour thinking about what you don't have.

Keep your mind on what you want. If you want more money, practice being thankful and happy about the money you do have. If you want more peace of mind, close your eyes for thirty seconds and remember a time when you felt peace and feel it all over again.

Coaching Assignment: Imagine that you had ten to

thirty percent less in your paycheck, or were in twice the debt you might be in now, and feel what that would be like. Then remind yourself of your current financial condition, which is better than the scenario you just imagined. Be grateful for what you have because gratitude will lead to other things you want in your life.

Focusing on our hurts, disappointments, mistakes and failures creates what I call "Emotional-Spiritual Cataracts." Cataracts in your physical eyes are a clouding of the lens in the eye that blurs your ability to see clearly. You want to have the vision to easily see all the wonder and opportunity around you.

I had a client who was told by his optometrist to come back in a year because he was beginning to develop cataracts in both eyes. One year went by without a visit to the optometrist, then two, then three. Five years later, when he eventually went to the doctor to get his eyes checked, he was told, "Because you didn't come to me earlier, your condition has worsened; you are legally blind."

Believe it or not, my client was shocked at the diagnosis. It had happened so gradually that he had not noticed the cloudiness of vision and the ever growing darkness he was living in. That's what can happen when we unknowingly focus on what's wrong with ourselves and our lives.

The light and fire of life begins to dim. Because it's often a slow and gradual process we don't even notice it. We can have "Emotional-Spiritual Cataracts" without knowing it or without knowing how much vision we've lost. It can happen to any of us when we let difficult experiences in life cloud our vision.

I know what it's like to be betrayed by a best friend and I know what it's like to have a business partner inflict serious harm on me and others before I knew what he had done. When I did find out about what had happened, I was devastated. I allowed these experiences to destroy my trust in most people and consume my life for a period of time.

Before I knew it, guilt, shame, fear and anger had taken

over. When that happens we have to decide what we're going to do next. We can allow our circumstances in life to consume and destroy us or we can deal with the pain and become wiser, more loving and more resilient.

It's a matter of perspective—as always. That might seem harsh, but it's the way it works. If you want to develop a stronger *gratitude consciousness*, start simple and keep at it until being aware of what you're grateful for is natural and easy. Why not stop right now and write down three things that you are thankful for (or three things that prompt a good feeling) no matter how small.

If you're having a really tough time in life right now and don't feel any gratitude when you write out your three things, that's fine. Do the exercise every day, whether you feel the gratitude or not—in time, it will come.

Coaching Assignment: You can get started right now, right here:

1) _____

2) _____

3) _____

If you haven't written three things out, please take a few seconds and do it now. If you want things to change, inwardly or outwardly, *you have to take action*. If you have already done the exercise, pause and notice the positive effects of doing something so simple.

Did it change everything and change all the tragedies in life? No, but it's a beginning, and practicing this simple habit will change your life. To continue to build on your gratitude consciousness, here are five things you can do:

1) Keep a daily gratitude journal:

This can be as easy as doing what you did above. Start your three things with "I am grateful for…" and finish the sentence. You can use other phrases such as "I am thankful for ___" or "I am happy about ___" or "This makes me feel good: ___."

What you write down can be anything from being thankful for your eyesight to feeling good about exercising that day or remembering a compliment someone gave you ten years ago. Nothing is too small or mundane to be grateful for. It's easier to boost your happiness than you think.

2) Write a thank you note:

Write a short thank you note or letter to someone who has touched your life in some way. E-mail is fine, but a handwritten note rocks. The time you take and the love you invest in your note or letter will probably make that person's day—and maybe yours as well.

From time to time, why not write a "Thank You" note or "Congratulations" note to yourself? Seriously. It might feel strange at first, but it will do wonders for you over time. Many of my clients find this uncomfortable at first—but this is a great way to develop a deeper sense of self-acceptance.

So what do you think—will you write yourself a note or letter? If not, stop and ask yourself why not? Why would you be willing to send someone else a thank you note or a note of congratulations—but not yourself? If you want your life to change for the better, learn how to give to yourself what you are so willing to give others. Learn to make giving yourself what you need and want a wonderful habit—you will love it.

3) Express appreciation to at least one person a day:

It doesn't matter if that person is a friend, a family member, a work colleague or a stranger. A simple "Thank you, I appreciate that" when someone compliments you or does something small for you will do—just be conscious of what you are doing.

You might tell someone what you see in them that you like, respect or appreciate. And guess what, the person you choose for the day can even be you. Ask yourself when was the last time you told yourself what you respect or appreciate about yourself—if you can't remember, that's a sign you are taking yourself for granted.

The great entrepreneur Mary Kay Ash, (Mary Kay Cosmetics) often said that when we are talking to someone, we should imagine a sign around their neck saying, "Make me feel important." That's a great idea and one you can apply to yourself. Imagine you have that sign around your neck and then express appreciation, respect and love to yourself.

4) Do something once a day for someone:

Doing something nice or helpful for someone, including yourself, is a way of expressing gratitude. Before and after you do whatever you decide to do, *tell yourself* you are doing it as a way of expressing your gratitude and to give back. Be intentional and conscious with this. Even if you are in the habit of doing something routine every day for a family member or for yourself, the key is to notice it and to *become more conscious of why you are doing it*—to express your gratitude.

My mom was in Costco one day with two of her younger grandchildren and they went to the food area to get pizza. When she went to pay for the food she found out they only took cash and she didn't have any. They told her to go to customer service and she could use her debit card.

However, she didn't have her debit card with her. Just then, another Costco employee, a young woman, came over and paid for the pizza and drinks. That made my mom's day, but I bet you it also made the young woman's day as well. A few days later my mom took homemade muffins to give to the employee, which she shared with her team at work. That made my mom feel good.

Here's what's amazing:: We can make someone's day and make our day at the same time simply by doing something kind or helpful for someone.

5) Think of something you are grateful for—then imagine what your life would be like *without* it.

It's easy to take what we have for granted—be it our possessions, our personal qualities, our relationships or anything else. Once we have something, we get used to it and we can easily lose the wonder and the gratitude we first felt. So imagine *not* having something—then recapture that great feeling of gratitude that you have it now.

Remember that **Gratitude Is the Great Happiness Multiplier** and it's the sixth secret to *Enlightened Happiness*. There are few things you can do to increase your joy, happiness and sense of fulfillment that are as simple as focusing on what you are thankful for. To develop your gratitude consciousness, here are some quotes to meditate upon:

"Be thankful for what you have; you'll end up having more. If you concentrate on what you don't have, you will never, ever have enough."
- Oprah Winfrey

"He is a wise man who does not grieve for the things which he has not, but rejoices for those which he has."
- Epictetus (Greek Philosopher, born a slave.)

"Let us rise up and be thankful, for if we didn't learn a lot today, at least we learned a little, and if we didn't learn a little, at least we didn't get sick, and if we got sick, at least we didn't die; so let us all be thankful."
- Buddha

"It is only with gratitude that life becomes rich."

SEVEN SECRETS TO ENLIGHTENED HAPPINESS

- Dietrich Bonhoeffer (1906-1945), Lutheran Minister

"When you arise in the morning, think of what a privilege it is to be alive." - Marcus Aurelius, Roman Emperor

"At times our own light goes out and it is rekindled by a spark from another person. Each one of us has cause to think with deep gratitude of those who have lighted the flame within us."
- Albert Schweitzer (1875-1965), Nobel Peace Prize-Winning Medical Missionary and Philosopher

"Silent gratitude isn't much use to anyone."
- Gladys Bronwyn Stern (1890-1920), Novelist

"Praise the bridge that carried you over."
- George Colman (1762-1836)

"Whatever you are truly grateful for and appreciate will increase in your life." - Srikumar S. Rao, Ph.D.

"Gratefulness is a force of energy and changes everyone it touches, beginning with self." - Alan Allard

SECRET SEVEN: ACTION FUELS YOUR HAPPINESS

"Action may not always bring happiness, but there is no happiness without action."
- William James, Ph.D.

Don't let what you cannot do stop you from doing what you can do."
- Legendary Basketball Coach John Wooden

"Success is the progressive realization of a worthwhile goal or ideal."
- Earl Nightingale

The seventh secret to *Enlightened Happiness* is **Action Fuels Your Happiness.** We are wired to act, to move forward and to achieve our goals and desires. Taking action on goals that are important to you is one of the quickest ways to boost your happiness—as long as you're doing what you want and enjoy the action you take.

As important as it is to know what you want, it is equally important to act on what you want because **until you take action, you are just wishing.** It's important to take action on your easier goals to gain confidence, otherwise you will keep some of your deeper desires safely tucked away in your subconscious mind. After all, there isn't a need for you to be conscious of them, since you are ignoring lesser goals and aspirations.

It's as if your subconscious mind says, "He isn't acting on the smaller things, so there's no reason to make him aware of the bigger things he wants. When he starts taking more action on the easier things, then he'll be ready for the bigger things."

We're focusing on action now because, for many people, there is a *knowing-doing gap* and our happiness gets hidden in that gap. What is that gap?

The knowing-doing gap is about failing to do what we know will help us build the ideal life we want. It happens when we think about taking a step towards what we want but then a conflicting belief or a conflicting desire stops us. Closing this gap more consistently will dramatically change your life.

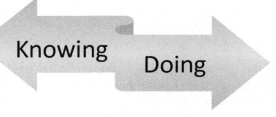

Action—or anything else—isn't *the* secret to your success, fulfillment and happiness. Yet your happiness depends upon you taking action towards your meaningful goals. Think about an area of your life that you have been thinking about—but not taking action on. What do you need to take action on or take more consistent action on?

Coaching Assignment: Make a list of action items and then prioritize what's on your list. You can do this for each area of your life, but choosing one and doing this exercise is a beginning:

1. _____

2. _____

3. _____

4. _____

5. _____

6. _____

7. _____

8. _____

9. _____

10. _____

Peter Drucker, perhaps the greatest management consultant of all time, said the greatest problem in his life and others wasn't in knowing what to do—but in *doing* what we know to do. That is certainly true of my corporate clients, small business clients and my life coaching clients. It's not that they don't know what to do—it's that aren't doing what they already know to do.

What is your "Knowing-Doing" gap? It could be saving money, exercising regularly, reading something constructive every day, telling your significant other how much they mean to you, improving your self-talk or making a list of your strengths, past achievements or goals. Choose something and get started.

The very act of getting started will inspire you and keep you going. When you want to make a change of any kind, there are two ways of going about it. You can launch a massive change effort and go "all in" or you can make "micro-changes" one small step at a time.

For instance, if you want to get healthier and leaner, you can begin a challenging exercise program, dramatically change what you are eating, start meditating, document your behavior in a journal, listen to a hypnosis audio or work with a hypnotherapist or a coach. Taking massive action can be very effective but it might not be the best strategy for you right now.

The other strategy, the "micro changes" strategy is where you make one small change to get healthier and keep at it until it's a habit. You might decide it would be easy and comfortable for you to only eat fruits or vegetables after six p.m. and you keep doing that until you are ready to add another healthy habit that would be easy and comfortable to do.

A few months later, you find that you have changed enough small and easy behaviors that make a real difference in reaching your health goals. If you are having difficulty getting started, *start small*. Why not make change easier and boost your odds of success? Check out your self-talk and make whatever adjustments you need to make—what are you saying to yourself about getting started? Your self-talk has to support you in taking action towards your goals.

I was working with a client years ago who wanted to "lose weight" (not a term I recommend to use in your self-talk because when you lose something, you want to find it again) and I asked her if she watched television at night. She thought I was going to ask her to cut back on watching her favorite television shows, but I didn't. I suggested she use the time during commercials to walk in place while lifting her knees and later to add jumping jacks and then pretend to be using a jump rope and so on.

Her immediate response was, "That won't work! I need to join a gym and get serious." My next question to her was, "How easy would that be for you to do? How motivated are you when you think of doing that?" She realized she didn't really want to do that; it was merely what she thought she "should" do.

Fortunately, she experimented with the "easy exercise during commercials" on small success led to another and another until she reached her health goal. Would you rather try to achieve success in one month and fail because you expected too much too soon or give yourself three months and succeed?

Sometimes, in order to take action, we need more support. Do you need more support in some way? Asking for support and using it is a form of taking action and takes its own brand of courage. Identify who can help and support you and call them to ask for what you need. Do you need help seeing the possibilities in the midst of your challenges? Take action and talk with someone that can help you shift your perspective.

Coaching is a form of support that has an immediate and long-term Return on Investment. That's why the sports world has used coaches for decades and it's why the business world has finally come on board. An effective coach won't cost you in the long run, but not having one will. If you don't believe that, you've never experienced a powerful coach.

I list action as a *secret* to happiness because when we're frustrated or discouraged we forget how powerful action and implementation is. There are plenty of intelligent people who flounder because they don't take action. They *know* but they don't *do* and they get stuck in their mind, so to speak. They overthink things. If you are overthinking things, it's time to focus more on taking action.

Coaching Assignment: Make a list of at least five to ten action steps you can take on a certain challenge or opportunity.

Coaching Assignment *Next Step*: Look at the ten action items you listed. *Then, pick the easiest one and get started.*

That will give you momentum and you will be in the game. Any action you take—no matter how small—is powerful because it sets you up for more success.

Remember that **success can generate even more success.** Also, remember that the smallest of actions is ten times more powerful than the action not taken. Honor yourself for taking the smallest of steps and then celebrate each step along the way—even if it's just to congratulate yourself. Then pick another step, however small, and take that step. You will create positive energy with each step you take.

Barbara is a client who is a freelance graphic designer and she wanted to gain new clients. She decided to call advertising agencies she had worked with in the past and did so over the course of a week. Barbara called me not long ago and reported that although she had some possible work that would come from the calls she had just made—nothing had materialized from them—yet.

What was interesting, though, was that three former clients she *hadn't* talked to in over two years called out of the blue to hire her again. Interesting, isn't it? It's amazing how when you give something, the Universe responds in kind.

Barbara didn't get work from the clients she called; yet the Universe/Spirit/God/Life (whatever term that is meaningful to you) responded to her action. If that thinking doesn't resonate with you, no big deal. Just take action and you will get results anyway.

Our actions set things into motion and are always rewarded; maybe not from the place we invest our energies, but from somewhere. As William Hutchison Murray wrote, **"Whatever you can do or dream you can, begin it. Boldness has genius, power and magic in it."**

It takes some amount of boldness to act, even if it's just a little bit. You don't have to be fearless; no one is. You don't have to be perfect; no one is. You don't even have to have it all figured out; none of us do. But, if you want to be happy, you do have to take *some* action on what is important to you.

I would say more, but I'll stop here so you can take some action. Why not start with the exercise above: Come up with ten things you can take action on to improve an area of your life, pick the easiest one and get started. Then move on to the next easiest item when you're ready.

Remember, the seventh secret to Enlightened Happiness is **Action Fuels Your Happiness.**

Here are some quotes on action to inspire and move you into action:

> *"Action is the foundational key to all success."*
> *- Pablo Picasso*

> *"Action is the real measure of intelligence."*
> *- Napoleon Hill*

> *"Action expresses priorities."*
> *- Mahatma Gandhi*

> *"There are risks and costs to action. But they are far less than the long range risks of comfortable inaction."*
> *- John F. Kennedy*

> *"An organization's ability to learn, and translate that learning into action rapidly, is the ultimate competitive advantage."*
> *- Jack Welch*

> *"Don't wait to feel motivated—take action now; your motivation will catch up with you."*
> *- Alan Allard*

BONUS CHAPTER: HOW TO RISE ABOVE YOUR CIRCUMSTANCES!

Have you ever wondered why some people roll with the punches in life—while others just get beat up? We could spend a lot of time discussing why that is so, but one thing is clear: how you view your challenges and setbacks determines what happens next.

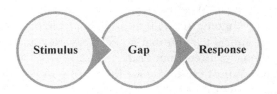

If you think of a challenge as the stimulus in the stimulus-response equation—between the stimulus and your response there is always a gap. In each gap between the stimulus and the response, you will discover the opportunity to choose your perspective and your response. Victor Frankl, M.D., makes this clear in his book, *Man's Search For Meaning*. Dr. Frankl was a Jewish psychiatrist who endured one of the most horrendous concentration camps during World War II. He learned in the harshest of times about our power to choose our beliefs and perspectives in life.

From Frankl's experience, we know happiness is a choice in the sense that our unhappiness or happiness comes from the perspectives and beliefs we choose to live from. Rising above your circumstances demands conscious awareness and thoughtful choices. Your happiness depends more on your state of mind and on you taking effective action than it does on your state of circumstances.

If you think you can change your circumstances, you probably will, and if you think you can't, you probably won't. You have to take charge of your perspective and your mindset because all change starts there. Remember, the *Universe works from the inside out.*

Mindset, attitude, belief system, perspective; whatever you want to call it, it explains a lot in life. Your mindset will tip the scales of happiness one way or the other—and your mindset is under your control.

I say mindset is everything even though genetics plays a role in happiness. But genetics isn't the deciding factor; your *mindset is*. More than that, your subconscious beliefs and your ongoing self-talk impacts your biology—because neuroscientists tell you that you can rewire your brain and your thoughts affect your body.

You cannot change your life until you change your mindset—your belief system. That's how important your mindset is. However, your mindset isn't just powerful; it is subject to your control. You are the only one who determines what your beliefs and perspectives will be. You have free will to determine what you think and what you believe.

Because that is so, you can increase your happiness levels. To do this, you have to understand that **how you feel about and react to your circumstances comes**

from your thoughts and beliefs about your circumstances; not directly from your circumstances.

Remember that your thoughts/self-talk leads to your emotions, your emotions leads to your decisions, your decisions leads to your behaviors and your behaviors leads to your results.

It's not that your circumstances don't matter; it's that your perspective and your self-talk matter more. That's why two people facing the same circumstances can respond very differently. They face the same situation but they tell themselves different "stories" about their situation.

One ends up being proactive and making progress and the other one ends up feeling dejected and defeated. Most of us, by far, have been taught that "good" circumstances make us happy and "bad" circumstances make us unhappy. At first glance, that makes sense. But it doesn't when you really examine the evidence.

Think back to when you were talking with a friend who was in a "bad mood." You listened and empathized with them, asked a question or two or made a comment, and somewhere along the way their mood shifted. What happened? It's deceptively simple—with your help, they changed their thinking, and therefore the level of consciousness they were operating from. It's amazing how that works.

There is one thing we know for sure: **Our thoughts lead to our emotions.** That means if we think depressing thoughts, we will feel depressed and if we think confident thoughts, we will feel confident. However, if we're weighed down with worry or depression, thinking confident or "positive" thoughts won't change everything instantly. We have to believe what we're thinking for it to have an effect. The reason someone is depressed is they believe what they're telling themselves—"Things are bad and they're not going to get better."

When I say our thoughts lead to our emotions, I'm talking about thoughts we give weight to and believe. That's the context of what the late Norman Vincent Peale wrote: **"Change your thoughts and you change your world."** Magic happens when we realize we can choose our emotions by choosing our thoughts, beliefs and perspectives. That realization gives us the power to change our lives and to change our destiny.

William James, considered to be the Father of American Psychology (1899-1944), wrote that he considered the greatest discovery of his generation to be this: **"Human beings, by changing the inner attitudes of their minds, can change the outer aspects of their lives."** Easier said than done? Yes.

Sometimes it's harder at times than others because some challenges are more difficult than others. Maybe you are in a tough situation right now and it's been getting the best of you. That's when you need what we're talking about the most. It might not always be easy, but it always pays off.

You can rise above your circumstances by rising above your old thoughts and beliefs—and you do that by thinking in new ways that empower and inspire you. Remember: Your circumstances matter, but your perspective matters more.

SEVEN SECRETS TO ENLIGHTENED HAPPINESS

WRAPPING UP

Happiness is created from the inside out, and while outer circumstances certainly influence us, they don't have to control us. You were meant to live a happy and fulfilling life but that doesn't mean it will happen without you consciously creating it. You have to create your happiness from within because *the universe works from the inside out.*

You will be happier when you make a commitment to yourself to use the *Seven Secrets to Enlightened Happiness*.

Secret One:
Your Beliefs Create Your Reality

Secret Two:
Your Inner Vision Is the Mental Blueprint For Your Future

Secret Three:
Master Your Self-Talk, Master Your Life

Secret Four:
Self-Confidence Fuels Your Success

Secret Five:
There Is No Substitute for Self-love

Secret Six:
Gratitude is the Great Happiness Multiplier

Secret Seven:
Action Fuels Your Happiness

You have taken action to achieve more happiness by reading this book—that's a great start. **Read this book over and over again, do the exercises, apply what you learn, and you will be amazed at the changes.** Remember that spaced repetition and action are keys to retaining what you learn, including how to be happier.

Your subconscious mind doesn't change just because you tell it to one or two times. Your subconscious mind is like a garden and you are the master gardener. You have to plant what you want in terms of your beliefs, your thoughts, your goals and your desires—and then you have to nurture and care for your mental, emotional and spiritual garden.

Each time you read this book, you are "tilling the soil" of your subconscious mind and nurturing the new beliefs and thought patterns you want to take root and grow.

Please let me know how this book has helped you. Email me at alan@alanallard.com (yes, you will hear back from me) or give me a call at 678-778-9012. If you have questions about life coaching, couples coaching, consulting, training or executive coaching for your organization, let's discuss your needs and opportunities.

You can find additional resources for help and information about my work as a life coach, corporate consultant, executive coach, speaker or trainer at www.alanallard.com.

I wish you all the happiness and success in the world - you truly deserve it.

MY GIFT TO YOU

I have a gift for you: A full coaching session where you will experience a breakthrough and go away with an action plan to keep the momentum going.

Why would I do this? Because telling you what coaching is like can't do it justice—you have to experience what powerful coaching is. Your coaching session is a gift from me to you. The only thing you need to commit to is one and a half to two hours for the coaching session. My experience has shown me that we need that time to dive deep enough to get to what we need to in order for you to experience a breakthrough.

Other than my website or my speaking and workshops, this is how I introduce people to my work—by allowing you to experience what powerful coaching is.

Call me at 678-778-9012 or email me at alan@alanallard.com to set your coaching time up.

SEVEN SECRETS TO ENLIGHTENED HAPPINESS

SUGGESTED RESOURCES

Rising Strong, Brene Brown (www.brenebrown.com)

Daring Greatly, Brene Brown

The Happiness Advantage, Shawn Achor

Before Happiness: The 5 Hidden Keys to Achieving Success, Spreading Happiness, and Sustaining Positive Change, Shawn Achor

The How of Happiness: A New Approach to Getting the Life You Want, Sonja Lyubomirsky

Real Happiness: The Power of Meditation, Sharon Salzberg

Creating Your Best Life: The Ultimate Life List Guide, Caroline Adams Miller, Michael Frisch

Man's Search for Meaning, Victor Frankl, M.D.

Shift your Mind, Shift the World, Steve Chandler

Nathaniel Branden, Ph.D. (Any of his books or audios)

Practical Wisdom, Frank Mallinder

Louise Hay (Any of her books or audios)

Eldon Taylor, Ph.D. (Any of his books or audios)

Helene Lerner (Any of her books or audios)

SEVEN SECRETS TO ENLIGHTENED HAPPINESS

ALAN ALLARD, Ph.D.

WHAT ALAN'S CLIENTS ARE SAYING

"Alan is an exceptional human behavior specialist. I use that phrase because the context whether coaching, speaking, or writing is just the outlet to the value he provides for those who engage him. You don't want to miss working him when a need arises! Each dollar you spend will have a return on investment 10 fold." -JoAnn Corley, CEO, The Human Sphere

"Working with Alan has been an incredible life-transforming experience. I am a completely different person and a much happier person since working with him. I don't know too many people that are as insightful and absolutely brilliant as he is. Since working with him, incredible pathways and opportunities have opened up for me, and I have the courage to take advantage of them."
-Steve Pederson, Musician/Songwriter

"As my personal coach, Alan has transformed my personal life and my business in ways that seem impossible to others." -Sarah Mitchell, Life Transformation Coach, Executive Coach, Trainer, Speaker (www.2ecoaching.com)

"Alan Allard is an exceptional executive coach, a skillful communicator and a highly effective facilitator of change. He has been the catalyst for significant personal growth and professional advancement in my life and in my vocation as a marketing professional. Most recently, I hired Alan as my executive coach. Our weekly coaching sessions over a very short span of time has led to a monumental paradigm shift in my personal fulfillment and the trajectory of my career.

Alan's skillful coaching led me to aggressively and confidently pursue a senior executive position at a Top 5 financial services company in the U.S.. Looking to find a right-fit job and a right-fit culture, I am now an integral member of a dynamic, innovative, employee-focused organization. Each were goals that Alan helped me to define, target, and acquire. Alan understands that maximizing performance begins with the alignment of clear goals, congruent values and useful beliefs.

He has the unique ability to help individuals optimize their self-confidence, clarify their vision, and re-tool their value system based upon useful beliefs. It takes a skilled coach to nurture inner confidence in order to bring about dramatic change in personal and professional performance. I will continue to recommend Alan without reservation or hesitation." - From Clete Thompson, VP of Marketing

"Alan's coaching has been key to me moving forward, not only in my career, but also in dramatically changing my personal life. I now have a new job at almost twice my previous income. Alan was the perfect 'GPS' that pinpointed exactly where I was and how to get to where I wanted to be. It is worth the time—and worth so much more than the investment." -Frank Cole, Sales Manager

"When I think about what great coaches do, they have one thing in common. They bring out the very best a person has to offer. Alan has a very keen ability to discover, unlock, and foster those talents within. His specific and customized approach has been extremely impactful in my life.

As a result of working with Alan, I have been the beneficiary of an increased level of confidence, much more effective communication and the ability to bring both my personal and professional life into high definition.

The most exciting results for me however, lie in the gains that have been produced within my relationships and ability to lead individuals in a large and complex environment.

In today's business when truly positive sustainable results are at a premium, I can think of nothing that has been more rewarding to that end than the coaching I have received from Alan." -Scott Watson, Regional Sales and Operations Manager

"When I was transitioning from the number two position to President and CEO of my organization, Alan's coaching and insight was great in helping me make that transition more successful." - From Doug Hart, Former President, SEU Local Union # 1, Chicago

"So how about coaching? Is it an effective way to get ahead? Can paying a business coach to talk with you over the phone really make a difference?

I must admit to having a small demon on my shoulder when it comes to coaching. It's probably a second cousin to the demon who whispers in my ear when confronted by a therapist. Part of me is just daring the person to utter that awful phrase, "How does that make you feel?"

Recently I went through a few months of coaching and here's the bottom line:

I will make twice as much during the second half of this year as I did during the first half. And next year is looking even better. So how does this weird magic work?

How can talking with a business coach make that kind of a difference? My coach was Alan Allard.

He's a patient man. I probably spent the first two sessions introducing him to my demon. After all, the guy used to be a therapist himself. And I think he came perilously close to asking me how I felt on a couple of occasions.

For the first few sessions at least, I had very little idea of what he was trying to do with me. I couldn't quite figure out the process he was following. As it turned out, that didn't really matter. In fact, the entire experience was like trying to grab hold of mist.

What he did, with his cauldron and frogs and eyes of newt, was re-awaken a level of self-confidence I had somehow lost. Not just in myself, but in my work. (And no, I had no idea I had lost that level of self-confidence. That realization came as quite a shock to me.)

Feeling good is one thing. Feeling good in a way that one can directly apply to one's work or business is quite another. In other words, he didn't just sugar coat me with a cloud of ethereal, feel-good encouragement. He gave me something I could take to the bank.

I have no idea when or how it happened, but he quietly opened a couple of doors deep inside me and then stood back and waited. And I guess that's his skill. To open or re-open doors. To enable people to tap into strengths and depths which they either never knew they had, or had somehow forgotten.

Perhaps Alan won't thank me for describing him in a pointy hat with a large cauldron. I use the analogy simply because I can't unravel the mystery of how he made his magic. All I know is that it worked.

So if you have a feeling that you're not moving ahead in your career as fast as you could, or that your freelance business should be booming, but isn't, consider engaging a business coach. And if you want to speak with Alan, he's a great coach and an outstanding person." - Nick Usborne,

ALAN ALLARD, Ph.D.

Author and Marketing Expert

"Best money we every spent! For many years I was a stay-at-home mom, working part time jobs. As our children started moving on with their lives, I found the need to redirect my life and follow a career in the theatre, which I had the education but little experience to accomplish. When I started meeting with Alan, I was working as a professional re-enactor for a living history program. Alan has helped me have the confidence to pursue my passion to be a successful theatre dresser and a costumer.

In a year's time, I have undergone a personal transformation in my thinking and as a result accept regular professional theatre "gigs". He is very intuitive and has helped me to think "outside the box." At the same time, my husband had become increasingly unhappy in his job and his health was suffering because of it. Alan was instrumental in helping my husband to change careers and be happy and fulfilled. Alan has also been equally valuable to my husband and I in addressing and encouraging us to change issues that had hindered our marriage for 20 years." -Beth Staff, M.A.

"Participating in your workshop, 'Creating Continual Patterns of Success' was refreshing and enlightening. The atmosphere was warm and genuine. I found your material to be cutting edge, and I wanted you to know that I began implementing ideas from your workshop immediately. Your grasp for the subject matter, humor and heartfelt stories made the workshop most interesting. I plan to attend other workshops presented by you in the future, and I have already told several colleagues about the workshop." -From Mark Sanders, Professional Speaker

SEVEN SECRETS TO ENLIGHTENED HAPPINESS

ABOUT ALAN

Alan Allard is a former psychotherapist, now an executive coach, consultant, speaker and life transformation coach. He works with individuals, couples and companies. Alan's clients have included The Centers for Disease Control, Evonik Corporation, Lucent Technologies, American Cyanamid, The U.S. Department of Agriculture, United Way and The Chicago Tribune.

Alan has conducted trainings and workshops throughout North America for employees from organizations such as The F.B.I., McDonald's, Hershey Hotel, Penske, Salvation Army, Louisiana State University and American Red Cross.

Alan has a Master's degree in Counseling from an accredited university and a Doctoral degree in Counseling from an unaccredited university. The master's degree allowed him to practice psychotherapy in the Chicago area for twelve years. The doctoral degree work expanded his thinking and life dramatically. His dissertation was on "Self-Transformation and Self-Hypnosis".

Sign up today for Alan's free "Coaching Minute" newsletter and blog at www.alanallard.com and get your free special report on "How to Thrive Under Pressure: Three Keys to Exceptional Performance at Work and In Life."

Made in United States
Orlando, FL
03 November 2021